formatio
TRADITION. EXPERIENCE.
TRANSFORMATION.

Formatio books from InterVarsity Press follow the rich tradition of the church in the journey of spiritual formation. These books are not merely about being informed, but about being transformed by Christ and conformed to his image. Formatio stands in InterVarsity Press's evangelical publishing tradition by integrating God's Word with spiritual practice and by prompting readers to move from inward change to outward witness. InterVarsity Press uses the chambered nautilus for Formatio, a symbol of spiritual formation because of its continual spiral journey outward as it moves from its center. We believe that each of us is made with a deep desire to be in God's presence. Formatio books help us to fulfill our deepest desires and to become our true selves in light of God's grace.

James Bryan Smith

The Good and Beautiful

GOD

FALLING IN LOVE WITH
THE GOD JESUS KNOWS

IVP Books

An imprint of InterVarsity Press
Downers Grove, Illinois

InterVarsity Press
P.O. Box 1400, Downers Grove, IL 60515-1426
World Wide Web: www.ivpress.com
E-mail: email@ivpress.com

InterVarsity Press® is the book-publishing division of InterVarsity Christian Fellowship/USA®, a movement of students and faculty active on campus at hundreds of universities, colleges and schools of nursing in the United States of America, and a member movement of the International Fellowship of Evangelical Students. For information about local and regional activities, write Public Relations Dept., InterVarsity Christian Fellowship/USA, 6400 Schroeder Rd., P.O. Box 7895, Madison, WI 53707-7895, or visit the IVCF website at <www.intervarsity.org>.

Scripture quotations, unless otherwise noted, are from the New Revised Standard Version of the Bible, copyright 1989 by the Division of Christian Education of the National Council of the Churches of Christ in the USA. Used by permission. All rights reserved.

Lyrics for "Boy Like Me/Man Like You" used by permission of David Mullins on behalf of Rich Mullins's family.

In some cases the names and situations of individuals described in this book have been changed to protect their privacy.

Design: Cindy Kiple
Images: Kevin Summers/Getty Images

ISBN 978-0-8308-3531-7

Printed in the United States of America ∞

Library of Congress Cataloging-in-Publication Data

Smith, James Bryan.
  The good and beautiful God: falling in love with the God Jesus knows / James Bryan Smith.
      p. cm.—(The apprentice series)
  Includes bibliographical references.
  ISBN 978-0-8308-3531-7 (cloth: alk. paper)
  1. God (Christianity)—Worship and love. 2. Spiritual life. I. Title.
  BV4817.S525 2009
  231.7—dc22

                                                                2009012144

P   23   22   21   20   19   18   17   16   15   14   13   12   11
Y   25   24   23   22   21   20   19   18   17   16   15   14   13   12   11   10

For my teachers

Dallas Willard and Richard J. Foster

Scribes of the kingdom who have brought
us treasures, old and new

MATTHEW 13:52

contents

introduction

When Jesus was asked what the greatest of all the commandments was, he quoted from the book of Deuteronomy: "'You shall love the Lord your God with all your heart, and with all your soul, and with all your mind.' This is the greatest and first commandment" (Matthew 22:37-38). In other words, the most important thing a human being does is to love God.

Do you remember mood rings? These were popular a long time ago. They changed color according to the mood of the wearer. (It was actually according to body temperature, but the sellers tried to pass it off as a mood change, and they made a lot of money; even some of mine.) What if someone made "love of God" rings that indicated the level of love the wearer feels for God? And what if everyone had to wear them? If dark blue was the color that indicated no love for God, and light blue was the color that indicated overflowing love for God, I imagine that a lot of people we see on the streets would have somewhat darkened rings on their fingers—and a lot of those people would even be Christians. To be honest, my own "love of God" ring would have been a rather washed-out blue had it not been for my good fortune. Thanks to God, I became the Forrest Gump of the Christian world.

MANY MARVELOUS MENTORS

In the movie *Forrest Gump*, the main character, Forrest, is an ordinary—somewhat challenged—man whose life is nothing special except that he has a good heart. Along the way, this "nobody" meets a lot of "somebodies." Forrest is an accidental bystander who stumbles into some of history's greatest moments (Dr. King's "I Have a Dream" speech) and greatest people (several U.S. presidents, celebrities, innovators). When I look back on my life, I feel like Forrest. I came from a Christmas-and-Easter-only Methodist family, and did not actually become a Christ-follower until my senior year of high school. I liked sports, pretty girls and Jesus—in that order. I was utterly average academically. I was literally three hundredth in a graduating class of six hundred. Not something to jazz up a resumé.

During my freshman year of college at a state university where I was playing sports and still pursuing pretty girls, Jesus began moving up the list. By the second semester he took over the top spot in my heart, so I decided to transfer to a Christian college. I chose a school called Friends University (I assumed they would be friendly at least) in Wichita, Kansas. I was an average student attending a small school in an out-of-the-way town, with no idea of what the future would hold. All I knew was that my yearning to know God was growing each passing day.

I did not know who Richard J. Foster was, or that he had written one of the most significant Christian books in the last hundred years (*Celebration of Discipline*). All I knew was that I had a class with him on Tuesdays and Thursdays from 10:30-12:00. He was unlike anyone I had ever known. He was really smart, but also funny. He loved to laugh, and he knew God in a way unlike anyone I had ever met—like he was a friend. He would teach me ways to know the God he knew.

Years later a mutual friend told me that Richard had been praying for a student to come along in whom he could invest his life and wisdom, and that apparently, not long after meeting me, he told this friend I was the one God had chosen for this Paul-and-Timothy-like mentoring. All I knew was that Richard was giving me additional reading assignments, praying with me, allowing me to babysit for him and his wife, and taking me on trips where he was speaking. It was during those personal times that I learned the most from him.

During my senior year, Richard connected me to Henri Nouwen, the great spiritual writer, as I was trying to decide which seminary to attend. At Henri's suggestion I applied to Yale Divinity School, and I got in. (Obviously, I had improved academically.) After seminary I served as a pastor in a local church, got married to Meghan, the prettiest and most down-to-earth girl I have ever seen (thank you, Jesus), learned some about how to lead a church, and found out quickly that being a pastor is really difficult. The one primary mission for a pastor should be to make disciples, but there are a thousand other pressing needs, problems and agendas that easily throw us off-track. Thankfully, my long association with Richard kept me focused on staying grounded in my own spiritual life.

A few years later I took a job teaching alongside Richard in the religion department at Friends University. While working as a professor I had another Forrest moment: a man named Rich Mullins, a famous Christian recording artist (he wrote and recorded "Awesome God" and "Step by Step"), took one of my classes. Having Rich in a class about God was like having Einstein in your math class—I was intimidated. But we became close friends, and eventually he lived in the attic apartment of our home for a little over two years. Through Rich I met Brennan Manning (author of *The Ragamuffin Gospel*). Brennan would also become a mentor and friend, and perhaps no one has taught me more about the love of God than he.

In 1987 Richard Foster invited me to help him build and launch a Christian spiritual renewal ministry called RENOVARÉ. He told me the name he had chosen for this ministry one day while eating a plate of spaghetti. No one could say the name or knew what it meant. We would spend the next twenty years, along with some other amazing men and women, traveling across the country leading conferences, retreats and seminars in an attempt to help people learn how to live a deeper, more balanced life with God. Some people thought we were "New Age" because of our funny name and because Richard used foreign terms like *contemplation* and *social justice*, and sometimes we were even picketed. Oh, the joys of serving Jesus!

Through Richard and Renovaré, I met Dr. Dallas Willard (author of *The Divine Conspiracy*), who teaches philosophy at the University of Southern California. I have never known anyone as brilliant as Dallas. He, like Richard, is a true disciple of Jesus. In 1994 Dallas invited me to coteach a class with him at Fuller Seminary in the doctor of ministry program. I accepted, and went on to teach that class with him for ten years. The class met for eight hours a day for two weeks each summer. I was just a glorified teaching assistant; Dallas taught 90 percent of the class. This meant that I was able to sit and listen to him teach for about seven hours a day over the course of ten days—about seventy hours. And I did this for ten years, which means I have heard Dallas teach on God, the kingdom of God, the Bible, the spiritual disciplines and life in general for over seven hundred hours!

Some of the finest teachers have poured their lives and their teaching into me, a nobody from nowhere, and I am most blessed. I suppose that is the way Christianity has worked from the beginning. Jesus took twelve nobodies on a three-year camping trip and invested his life in them because he believed in them. The influence of all of these people—Richard, Henri, Rich, Brennan and Dallas—on me is so strong that I am not sure I have any ideas that were not shaped by theirs. Their fingerprints are all over the book you are holding. I have studied all of their books, listened to their sermons, songs and lectures on tapes and CDs, but I can honestly say that it has been the one-on-one time spent with each of them that has influenced me the most. The long hikes with Richard, letters exchanged with Henri, nightlong discussions with Rich Mullins, lingering dinners with Brennan and ice-cream-eating sessions with Dallas (he likes vanilla—who orders plain vanilla?) are deeply imbedded into my soul.

HOW THIS BOOK CAME TO BE

This book is the culmination of twenty-five years of learning from these great men. In particular, the idea for this book started soon after I began working with Dallas. He kept talking about the need to create "a curriculum for Christlikeness" for individuals and churches. His blueprint for such a curriculum can be found in the ninth chapter of his great book *The Divine Conspiracy*. Even as he was developing that chapter, I kept pressing him with the question, "Can this really be done, Dallas?" He would say, "Yes, of course." Then I would ask, "Why don't you do it?" and he would say each time, "Because I think you should do it, Jim."

No pressure.

In 1998 I began creating a curriculum based on Dallas's simple blueprint for a course in learning to live as Jesus taught us to live. In 2003 I went to the church leadership board of the church where I attend (Chapel Hill United Methodist Church, Wichita, Kansas) and asked them if I could invite some people in the church to go through this curriculum with me. They eagerly agreed, and the first year I led twenty-five people through the thirty-week course. Midway through that year I began to suspect that Dallas was right all along. Genuine transformation into the character of Christ really is possible.

Since that time I have led another seventy-five people through it, and the results have always been the same: significant life change. In church, spouses come up to me and say, "What are you doing to my husband—he is a different person! He is more patient and more attentive to our whole family than ever before. I don't know what is going on, but you can be sure I am taking the course next year." In addition, this curriculum has been used by high school students in youth groups and college students on campus. When people ask me who the target audience is for this material, I always say, "Anyone who longs for change—young or old, new Christian or mature Christian, male or female, it doesn't matter."

THE BEGINNING OF A SERIES

The book you have in your hand is the first book in The Apprentice Series, which along with two other books form a "curriculum for Christlikeness." The aim of this first book is to help people discover the God Jesus revealed.

Each chapter deals with false concepts and the true one, namely, the narrative of Jesus. Each chapter also contains a soul-training exercise to help imbed the narrative of Jesus more deeply into our minds, bodies and souls. These exercises are not meant to make you more religious or impress God. They are meant to help you see and understand the world as Jesus did. At the end of the chapter there is a page that highlights the main ideas in the chapter. Throughout each chapter are questions that can be used for individual reflection or group interaction and discussion.

This book is titled *The Good and Beautiful God* because the focus is on the character of God and how we move into a life of intimacy with God. The second book in The Apprentice Series is titled *The Good and Beautiful Life*, which introduces the reader to the kingdom of God and focuses on our inward character, dealing specifically with the vices that cause ruin: anger, lust, lying, worry, judging others and so on. Following the Sermon on the Mount, this second book will look at the narratives behind these character flaws (for example, What are the narratives that lead to anger?) and will replace those narratives with Jesus' narratives about life in the kingdom of God. As with this book, each chapter will contain an exercise that is aimed at helping imbed the proper narrative into our souls.

The third book in this series is titled *The Good and Beautiful Com-*

munity. The focus of this book is to help us learn how to live as apprentices of Jesus in our ordinary, everyday lives. How do I live out Jesus' kingdom vision in my family? What impact will my life with God have on my life at work? In what ways can I, as a Christ-follower, change the world I live in? What will loving my enemies and blessing those who curse me look like in my daily life? Ultimately it all comes down to this: "the only thing that counts is faith working through love" (Galatians 5:6), at home, at work, in our community and on our planet.

But it all starts with knowing the God Jesus knows, and loving God with every fiber of your being. This is the spring and the foundation of the other two books, and in fact the entire Christian life. This may be the only book you read in this series, and if so, I pray that somehow your "love of God" ring brightens.

HOW TO GET THE MOST OUT OF THIS BOOK

This book is intended to be used in the context of a community—a small group, a Sunday school class, or a few friends gathered in a home or coffee shop. Working through this book with others greatly magnifies the impact. If you go through this on your own, only the first four suggestions below will apply to you. No matter how you use it, I am confident that God can and will accomplish a good work in you.

1. Prepare. Find a journal or notebook with blank pages.
You will use this journal to answer the questions sprinkled throughout each chapter and for the reflections on the soul-training experience found at the end of each chapter.

2. Read. Read each chapter thoroughly.
Try not to read hurriedly, and avoid reading the chapter at the last minute. Start reading early enough in the week so that you have time to digest the material.

3. Do. Complete the weekly exercise(s).

Engaging in exercises related to the content of the chapter you have just read will help deepen the ideas you are learning and will begin to mold and heal your soul. Some of the exercises will take more time to complete than others. Be sure to leave plenty of time to do the exercise before your group meeting. You want to have time not only to do the exercise but also to do the written reflections.

4. Reflect. Make time to complete your written reflections.

In your journal go through the questions posed throughout and at the end of each chapter. This will help you clarify your thoughts and crystallize what God is teaching you. It will also help with the next part.

5. Interact. Come to the group time prepared to listen and to share.

Here is where you get a chance to hear and learn from others' experiences and insights. If everyone takes time to journal in advance, the conversation in the group time will be much more effective. People will be sharing from their more distilled thoughts, and the group time will be more valuable. It is important to remember that we should listen twice as much as we speak! But do be prepared to share. The other group members will learn from your ideas and experiences.

6. Encourage. Interact with each other—outside of group time.

One of the great blessings technology brings is the ease with which we can stay in touch. It is a good idea to send an encouraging e-mail to at least two others in your group between meeting times. Let them know you are thinking of them, and ask how you can pray for them. This will strengthen relationships and deepen your overall experience. Building strong relationships is a key factor in making your experience a success.

one

what are you seeking?

Would you like to have abiding peace? Would you like to have a heart that is filled with love? Would you like to have the kind of faith that sees everything—even your failures and losses—in light of God's governance for good? Would you like to have the kind of hope that endures even in discouraging circumstances?

If this is the life you most deeply desire, then this book is meant for you.

A lot of people want to change and would answer yes to these questions, but many of them do not believe it is possible. After years of trying and failing, they lead a Christian life of quiet desperation, longing for change and yet certain it will never happen. So they sit in their pews each week, sighing silently, resigned to their fate.

I used to think that way. I tried and tried and tried to change. I prayed and prayed, pleading with God, begging God to change me. All to no avail. I wanted to become the kind of person Jesus described in the Sermon on the Mount—a person who loved his enemies and never worried about anything. But when I looked into my own heart, I discovered that I not only did not love my enemies, I didn't even love some of my friends, and I worried about everything.

Change came when, through two gifted mentors, I learned that transformation happens through training my soul. Richard Foster's understanding of how the spiritual disciplines work and Dallas Willard's understanding of how we interact with the kingdom of God are unsurpassed. The passion of my life has been to find the answer to this question: How do we become like Christ?

Describe your own experience with trying (and perhaps failing) to change. Could it be that the problem was not a lack of effort, but a lack of proper training? Explain.

I have come to believe that the problem is not that we do not want to change, nor is the problem that we are not trying to change. The problem is that we are not training. We have never been taught a reliable pattern of transformation.

PEACE AND JOY IN AN AIRPORT

Craig is one of the people who took part in the experiment in developing a curriculum for Christlikeness. After being involved in an apprentice group, Craig began to notice some real changes in his life in the way he behaved toward his family, friends and coworkers. He is a zoo architect, which requires him to travel a lot. One day he and his business colleague were flying back to the United States from Germany when they got stuck in the Atlanta airport and were told their flight home would be delayed several hours. Those several hours passed, and a few hours more, and then finally they were told the flight had been cancelled. The delay meant that there were no options to get home that night, and they would have to spend the night in Atlanta.

The anger level in the concourse was reaching a fever pitch. All of the passengers were forced into a long line to rebook their flights. Craig and his business partner stood in line and watched as each person spoke harshly to the young woman who was trying to help them. When it was Craig's turn, he looked at the young woman, smiled and said, "I promise I am not going to be mean to you." Her countenance softened, and she said softly, "Thank you." Their exchange was pleasant, and he got their flights booked for the next day. As they walked down the concourse, Craig was smiling despite the disappointment. His business partner had been watching him. He said, "Craig, I have known you for a long time. A year ago you would have been enraged by what we went through today, and you would have lit into that woman at the counter."

Craig said, "You know what, you're right. But I have changed. I know who I am, and I know where I am. I am a person in whom Christ dwells, and I live in the kingdom of a God who loves me and is caring for me. I'm frustrated, but I'm still at peace. We'll get home tomorrow. There's nothing for us to do. Anger doesn't help anything. I figure we might as well enjoy this unexpected turn of events."

His friend just shook his head in amazement. "I'm not sure what you've been eating or drinking, but you have really changed."

It was what Craig had been *doing* and *thinking* for the last year that brought about the change. Craig had followed his desire to become a different kind of person by signing up for the apprentice group and training for transformation. Craig was not alone. His desire to do the work, and the changes he experienced as a result, occurred only because of the work of the Holy Spirit.

Not by his own willpower.

FALSE NARRATIVE: WE CHANGE BY OUR WILLPOWER

When people decide to change something, they muster their "willpower" and set about trying to change some behavior. This nearly always fails. Approximately 95 percent of New Year's resolutions are broken by the end of January. Most people assume, when they fail to keep their resolution, that they did not have enough willpower. They think of themselves as weak and feel badly about their failure.

That is unfortunate. The reason they failed was not a lack of willpower. In fact, the will actually has no power. The will is the human capacity to choose. *Should I wear a red shirt or a blue one?* we ask ourselves. Ultimately we choose the blue one, and our will is the hinge on which the decision is made. But the will does not actually do anything. If I could look inside you to find your will, I would never find it. It is not next to your gallbladder! It is not an organ or a muscle that can grow or atrophy.

The will is more like a beast of burden that simply responds to the impulses of others. A horse does not choose where to go, but goes in whatever direction the rider tells it to go. The will works like that. Instead of one rider, it has several. The three primary influencers on the will are the mind, the body and the social context. First, what we think in our minds will in turn create emotions, which leads to decisions or actions. Second, the body is a complex inner working of impulses that influence the will. Most of our bodily system runs without our help, but when the body has a need (food, water) it expresses itself to the mind through feelings (hunger, thirst) and alerts the mind to send a message to the will: *Get food now.* Finally, the will is also influenced by our social context. We are highly influenced by the people around us. We call this "peer pressure."

The will is neither strong nor weak. Like a horse, it has only one task: to do what the rider (the mind, influenced by the body and the social realm) tells it to do. Therefore, change—or lack thereof—is not an issue of the will at all. Change happens when these other influencers are modified. The good news is that we have control over those other influencers. When new ideas, new practices and new social settings are adopted, change happens.

JESUS' NARRATIVE: WE CHANGE BY INDIRECTION

Jesus understood how people change. That is why he taught in stories. He used narrative to explain his understanding of God and the world: "The kingdom of God is like a mustard seed." "A man had two sons . . ." If we adopt Jesus' narratives about God, we will know God properly and right actions will follow. And the opposite is true. We change not by mustering up willpower but by changing the way we think, which will also involve changing our actions and our social environment. We change indirectly. *We do what we can in order to enable us to do what we can't do directly.* We change by the process of indirection.

Peyton Manning practiced indirection. He was the winning quarterback of Super Bowl XLI. It was a rainy night, and the ball was slippery. Rex Grossman, the quarterback for the losing team, fumbled several times. But Peyton Manning never fumbled. A few weeks after the Super Bowl a reporter discovered that every few weeks during the year Manning has his center (the one who snaps him the ball), Jeff Saturday, snap him water-soaked footballs. He practices handling wet footballs so he will be ready in case it rains—even though his team plays half of their games in a dome. Manning did what he could do (practice handling wet footballs over and over) to enable him to do what he could not without this preparation (play great in the rain).

We cannot change simply by saying, "I want to change." We have to examine what we think (our narratives) and how we practice (the spiritual disciplines) and who we are interacting with (our social context). If we change those things—and we can—then change will come naturally to us. This is why Jesus said his "yoke" was easy. If we think the things he thought, do the things he did and spend time with likeminded people, we will become like him, and it will not be difficult. If someone had asked Peyton Manning after the Super Bowl, "So, was it hard handling that wet football?" he would have likely said, "No. I practice that all the time when no one is watching." That is the perfect illustration of indirection.

I believe there is a reliable method of changing our hearts. It is not complicated, nor is it difficult. It does not rely on willpower. We begin with the triangle of transformation. It involves four basic elements: (1) changing the stories in our minds, (2) engaging in new practices (3) in reflection and dialogue with others who are on the same path, (4) all under the leading of the Holy Spirit.

Figure 1. The four components of transformation

STEP ONE: CHANGING OUR NARRATIVES

We are creatures who live by our stories. From early on we are told stories by our parents, which help us interpret how life is or how life ought to be. We are naturally drawn to stories and must follow them to their conclusion because stories are exciting. Jesus taught primarily in story form. One reason might be that stories are memorable. We may not be able to remember many (or any) of the Beatitudes, but we all can remember the story of the prodigal son.

When we have a significant experience—one that shapes us—we turn it into a story. For example, a powerful experience from childhood may have been a special birthday party where you got the gift you had been hoping for. You do not remember the event in exact detail. You remember it as a narrative—who was there, what was said, how you felt, what the cake looked like.

Narrative is "the central function . . . of the human mind." We turn everything into a story in order to make sense of life. We "dream in narrative, day-dream in narrative, remember, anticipate, hope, despair, believe, doubt, plan, revise, criticize, construct, gossip, learn, hate and love by narrative." In fact, we cannot avoid it. We are storied creatures. Our stories help us navigate our world, to understand right and wrong, and to provide meaning ("So the moral of the story is . . .").

There are all kinds of narratives. _Family_ narratives are the stories we learn from our immediate families. Our parents impart to us their worldview and their ethical system through stories. Key questions such as Who am I? Why am I here? Am I valuable? are answered early on in the form of narrative. There are _cultural_ narratives that we learn from growing up in a particular region of the world. From our culture we learn values (what is important, who is successful) in the form of stories and images. Americans, for example, are taught the value of "rugged individualism" through the stories of our past (the Revolution, the pioneers). There are _religious_ narratives—stories we hear from the pulpit, the classroom and religious books that help us understand who God is, what God wants of us and how we ought to live. Finally, there are _Jesus'_ narratives, the stories and images Jesus tells to reveal the character of God.

> What comes to mind as you read about narratives that have formed your way of thinking about the world? *How incredible that people w/ completely*

We are shaped by our stories. In fact, our stories, once in place, determine much of our behavior without regard to their accuracy or helpfulness. Once these stories are stored in our minds, they stay there largely unchallenged until we die. And here is the main point: these narratives are running (and often ruining) our lives. That is why it is crucial to get the right narratives.

Once we "find" the narratives inside our minds, we can measure them against Jesus' narratives. Because Jesus is the preexistent and eternal Son of God, no one knows God or the nature and meaning of

different family, cultural + Religious narratives (or NO Religious Narratives) Become one after Jesus NTvs. adopting life more than Jesus. Jesus' narratives are the truth. He himself is the truth. So the key is adopting Jesus' narratives.

Jesus revealed his Father to us. The New Testament reveals a God who is pulsing with goodness and power and love and beauty. To know the God of Jesus is to know the truth about who God really is.

In order to change we first have to change our minds. Jesus' opening line to his first sermon was, "Repent *[metanoia]*, for the kingdom of God is at hand." *Metanoia* refers to the changing of one's mind. Jesus understood that transformation begins in the mind. The apostle Paul said the same thing when he proclaimed, "Do not be conformed to this world, but be transformed by the renewing of your *minds*, so that you may discern what is the will of God—what is good and acceptable and perfect" (Romans 12:2, italics added).

Our family, cultural and even religious narratives might have their roots in the kingdom of this world. As Christ-followers we are called to "set [our] minds on things that are above" (Colossians 3:2). Most of all, we are called to have the very mind of Jesus: "Let the same mind be in you that was in Christ Jesus" (Philippians 2:5). Adopting Jesus' narratives is a way we come to have the mind of Christ. Once we get the right narratives in place, change will begin. But getting the ideas and information right is only the beginning.

STEP TWO: PRACTICING SOUL-TRAINING EXERCISES

Once we have the right narratives in place, we need to deepen them in the rest of our lives through specific activities that are aimed at making the narratives real not only to our minds but to our bodies and souls. You can call these activities "spiritual disciplines," but I prefer to call them "soul-training exercises." The reason for this is because the spiritual disciplines are actually not spiritual at all. Thinking they are "spiritual" leads people to practice them as isolated activities that are done in an attempt at making a person more "spiritual," whatever that means. They are done with no specific aim, and are often done legalistically to gain the favor of God or others.

The spiritual disciplines are *wisdom*, not *righteousness*. But they are wise practices that train and transform our hearts.

Athletes understand the necessity of training. They run and lift weights and practice over and over so that they can perform naturally, easily and with strength in competition. Paul compared our Christian life to the training of an athlete in several passages (1 Corinthians 9:25; 1 Timothy 4:7-8; 2 Timothy 2:5). In the same way, when we engage in the spiritual disciplines as *soul-training* exercises, we are doing so to change how we live.

> Have you practiced spiritual exercises (such as prayer, Bible reading or solitude) in your life, and if so, with what intention and what result?

The spiritual disciplines are meant to have a therapeutic effect. People who undergo *physical therapy* engage in exercises such as stretches and limb lifts to improve their ability. The way we practice these soul-training exercises should be the same. We do these things (even if they hurt a bit) because we want to improve how we function. They are an essential part of our soul transformation.

STEP THREE: PARTICIPATING IN COMMUNITY

Human beings are community-dwellers. Just as the eternal Trinity (Father, Son and Spirit) live in community, so also we who are made in God's image are meant to live and love in community. Unfortunately, however, spiritual formation is often approached as a very individualistic endeavor. We may tend to think of our spiritual growth as a personal pursuit, and not a communal activity.

Spiritual formation happens most profoundly in the context of a group. Participating in a group allows the influence of others to spur us on and encour-

> What has been your experience of Christian fellowship or community?

age us (Hebrews 10:24). The best way to use this book to make a complete and lasting change is to go through it with others. Of course, you can read it on your own and do the exercises as you please, but my field-testing of this material reveals that the solo approach has less of an impact.

STEP FOUR: THE WORK OF THE HOLY SPIRIT

The Holy Spirit is often the member of the Trinity that gets the least attention. We pray to God the Father, and when we read about Jesus in the Gospels we can picture him in human form. But the Holy Spirit is not often the focus of our lives.

I have come to believe that the Holy Spirit is not upset about this. The constant aim of the Spirit is to point us to the Father and the Son, and not to himself. Everything that happens to us in our Christian lives, however, is the work of the Holy Spirit. We become discontented with our lives, and it is the Spirit who gently nudges us toward Jesus. The Holy Spirit orchestrates the events of our lives with the single aim of making us disciples of Jesus. The Holy Spirit is at work in our lives in subtle ways, ways we cannot often discern. But the Spirit is at work nonetheless. The components of change happen when the Holy Spirit is at work in the midst of them.

The Holy Spirit and narratives. Jesus told his disciples that upon his departure and ascension God the Father would send the Spirit to be their guide: "But the Advocate, the Holy Spirit, whom the Father will send in my name, will teach you everything, and remind you of all that I have said to you" (John 14:26). The Holy Spirit is our unseen teacher who points us to Jesus and reminds us of his words. In this sense, the Holy Spirit is the one who is helping us change our narratives to Jesus' narrative. He leads us away from false narratives and replaces them with true narratives: "When the Spirit of truth comes, he will guide you into all the truth" (John 16:13).

Even our conversion is dependent on the work of the Holy Spirit: "No one can say 'Jesus is Lord' except by the Holy Spirit" (1 Corinthians 12:3). Our decision to follow Jesus and accept him as Lord and Savior is only possible because the Holy Spirit has guided us into this truth. When we replace a wrong narrative, such as "God is an angry judge who is poised to punish us," with Jesus' narrative that God is a loving "Abba," that too is the work of the Holy Spirit.

Paul notes, "When we cry, 'Abba! Father!' it is that very Spirit bearing witness with our spirit that we are children of God" (Romans 8:15-16). I love that phrase—the Spirit *bears witness* with our spirit. The Spirit changes our false narratives by bearing witness to the truth. The two most important relationships we have are our relationship with Jesus as Lord (Greek *kyrios*), and our relationship with God as our Father (*Abba* in Aramaic, the language Jesus spoke). We come to know Jesus as our Lord and God as our Abba only by the work of the Spirit who offers us these narratives of truth.

The Spirit and soul training. The Spirit comes alongside us, within us and around us as we engage in spiritual exercises. Every soul-training exercise we engage in would be of no value if it were not for the work of the Holy Spirit. When we open the Bible and begin to read slowly and listen for God, the Spirit illumines our mind and gives us a direct word from God. Even prayer, which we often think we initiate, is really the work of the Holy Spirit: "Likewise the Spirit helps us in our weakness; for we do not know how to pray as we ought, but that very Spirit intercedes with sighs too deep for words" (Romans 8:26). When we pray, we do not pray alone. The Spirit has subtly prompted us to pray, preceding us in prayer, and then prays with and for us.

When we practice solitude or silence, when we engage in service or simplicity, it is the Spirit who is aiding us and encouraging us. When we come to a new discovery or awareness during our time of prayer or reflection in our journals, once again it is the Spirit who is whispering truths that transform us. This is not easy to detect, and often we only hear the echoes of the Spirit, but as we give ourselves more and more to God through these soul-training exercises, our ability to hear increases. Still, all of these exercises and activities would be worthless were it not for the presence and work of the Holy Spirit.

The Holy Spirit and community. The Holy Spirit is like a symphony conductor, orchestrating our communal life of prayer and worship and praise. But unlike a human conductor, the Holy Spirit endows each of us with gifts and graces that are meant to be used for the benefit of others (see 1 Corinthians 12). When we hear a sermon that touches our hearts, the Spirit is at work not only in inspiring the preacher but in softening our hearts and opening our ears.

In the book of Acts we see the Holy Spirit in every story as the early Christian community learns how to live together and participate in the ministry of Jesus. One of my favorite stories is about how the Spirit prompted the community to commission Barnabas and Saul (Paul) to go on a mission: "While they were worshiping the Lord and fasting, the Holy Spirit said, 'Set apart for me Barnabas and Saul for the work to which I have called them.' Then after fasting and praying they laid their hands on them and sent them off" (Acts 13:2-3). Notice the context: they were together (community) worshiping and fasting (engaging in spiritual disciplines) when the Spirit spoke to them. The Spirit could have spoken directly to any one of them, but instead chose to speak to the community. Then they laid hands on Barnabas and Paul and sent them off.

> How do you see the Holy Spirit interacting with the three other components of change?

When we gather together in Christian fellowship, the Holy Spirit is once again at work, often imperceptibly, with the single intention of leading us to a deeper love of Jesus and the Father. When I was leading one group through this material, I felt prompted to stop and use the last fifteen minutes of our hour together simply to pray with one another in small groups of three. I encouraged the people to share a bit about what they would like prayer for and then spend a few minutes praying for those specific needs. Within only a few minutes I looked around and heard people sobbing. We had been together for about fifteen weeks, but it was only when we opened ourselves up to one another and let the Spirit lead us that real community began to occur.

TRANSFORMATION: THE FRUIT OF THE SPIRIT

What Craig demonstrated in the Atlanta airport was none other than the fruit of the Spirit. Paul offers us a list of virtues that come into our lives as a result of the work of the Spirit: "The fruit of the Spirit is love, joy, peace, patience, kindness, generosity, faithfulness, gentleness, and self-control" (Galatians 5:22-23). We cannot grit our teeth and become patient. We cannot muster our willpower and become kind. We cannot stress and strain our way to generosity. This "fruit" is the work of the Holy Spirit. Like the fruit on a tree, it is developed naturally from the inside to the outside.

When the Spirit has changed our narratives sufficiently, we begin to think differently. As a result we begin to believe in and trust a good and loving God who is strong and powerful. We begin to see how Jesus lived a perfect life that we cannot live and offered that life to the Father on our behalf, setting us free from having to earn God's love and favor. And as we engage in soul-training exercises—especially in the context of community—our confidence that God is at work in and among us increases. This creates an inward change that manifests itself in outward behavior.

Now, when faced with an airport delay, we can take a deep breath and remember who we are. Like Craig, we can endure these trials with love, joy, peace, patience and kindness.

COME AND SEE

I love the story of how Jesus meets two of his first disciples. They had been disciples of John the Baptist, but John encouraged them to follow Jesus. When Jesus discovers they are shadowing him, he stops and asks a telling question. "'What are you looking for?' They said to him, 'Rabbi' (which translated means Teacher), 'where are you staying?' He said to them, 'Come and see.' They came and saw where he was staying, and they remained with him that day" (John 1:38-39).

Jesus simply asks what they are seeking. This is such an important question, one we should ask ourselves over and over. What is it that you really want? What we truly desire, what we are most passionate about, will determine how we organize our lives.

Notice the strange and illogical answer—"Rabbi, where are you staying?"—the disciples give to Jesus' simple question, "What are you looking for?" Jesus, however, knows their hearts. They are following him because they are passionate about living a good and beautiful life, and they are hoping Jesus will lead them to it. Jesus answers with a simple yet profound answer: "Come and see." He answers both questions—the one about where he is residing, and the one about what they are most seeking. He knows that if they follow him they will find what they truly want in life.

Jesus has called you to be one of his disciples. I know this because you are reading this book. The Holy Spirit has led you thus far through your desire for a deeper life, a more authentic faith and a more certain hope in the God Jesus knows. Jesus has invited you to become one of his apprentices. This is not because of your strength or skills, but because he knows that if you learn how to think as he thinks and to do the kinds of things that he did, you can live an amazing life. You may not move mountains or walk on water, but I have confidence that you can begin to learn how to be patient and kind, how to forgive those who have hurt you, and how to bless and pray for your enemies. That is just as miraculous as walking on water.

May you fall in love with the God Jesus knows.

sleep

The number one enemy of Christian spiritual formation today is exhaustion. We are living beyond our means, both financially and physically. As a result, one of the primary activities (or anti-activities) of human life is being neglected: sleep. According to numerous studies, the average person needs approximately eight hours of sleep in order to maintain health. This tells me that God has designed humanity to spend nearly one-third of our lives sleeping. This is a stunning thought. We were made to spend a large portion of our existence essentially doing nothing. The failure to do so results in damage to physical health, loss of energy and decreased productivity. And our sleep deprivation often hurts others. More people are killed each year by *drowsy* drivers than by drunk drivers.

In Dr. Siang-Yang Tan's excellent book *Rest*, he quotes Arch Hart, who says simply, "we need rest more today than ever before in history." Dr. Tan goes on to show how in the 1850s the average American slept 9.5 hours a night. By 1950 that number dropped to eight hours a night. Today the average American sleeps under seven hours a night. We have dropped under the needed amount of sleep, and we are suffering for it on several levels. A poll done by the National Sleep Foundation showed that 49 percent of American adults have sleep-related problems, and that one in six suffers from chronic insomnia. A physician friend told me that the most frequent prescriptions she writes for her patients are for sleeping problems.

In contrast, a study was done by the National Institute of Mental Health in which participants were allowed to "sleep as much as they could" each night, and on average people slept 8.5 hours. Those who participated in the study said they felt happier, less fatigued, more creative, energetic and productive. God designed us to be stewards of our lives—body, mind and soul. We must begin with caring for our bodies, which apparently require seven to eight hours of sleep each night. To fail to do so obviously results in fatigue and, consequently, failure in other areas of our lives.

What does this have to do with Christian spiritual formation? The human person is not merely a soul housed in a body. Our bodies and souls are unified. If our bodies suffer, so do our souls. We cannot neglect the body in pursuit of spiritual growth. In fact, neglecting our bodies necessarily impedes our spiritual growth. Everything we do in our lives, including the practices of spiritual formation, we do in and with our bodies. If our bodies are not sufficiently rested, our energies will be diminished and our ability to pray, read the Bible, enter solitude or memorize Scripture will be minimized.

The focus of this chapter has been to show how spiritual formation is a combination of our action and God's action. We must *do* something, but we rely on God to provide what is needed in order to change. Sleep is a perfect example of the combination of discipline and grace. You cannot make yourself sleep. You cannot force your body to sleep. Sleep is an act of surrender. It is a declaration of trust. It is admitting that we are not God (who never sleeps), and that is good news. We cannot make ourselves sleep, but we can create the conditions necessary for sleep.

I have stressed that the disciplines are not ways to earn anything from God, but wise practices that allow God to teach, train and heal us. Sleep, therefore, is a kind of "anti-discipline" discipline. Begin with this exercise and continue practicing it throughout the time you work through this material (and, I hope, for the rest of your life). You will never come to a point where you are above the need for adequate sleep.

THE DISCIPLINE OF SLEEP

At least one day this week sleep until you cannot sleep any more. If you need to, find a day when you can sleep in. Your aim is to sleep, or to stay in bed, until you can finally say, I am completely rested. I do not need to sleep or stay in bed a minute longer. You may need to solicit the help of others if you have family members who need your care.

If you are unable to do this exercise, try another: aim to get at least seven hours of sleep at least three times this week. This may require going to bed earlier than usual. The following are some tips to help you fall asleep:

1. Go to sleep at a consistent time each night.

2. Try not to engage in activities that increase stress (such as, perhaps, watching TV or spending time on the computer) right before bedtime.

3. If you are affected by stimulants (caffeine, spicy foods) avoid them in the evening.

4. Do not force yourself to fall asleep. If you do not feel drowsy, read a book, meditate on a psalm, listen to soft music, or sit up and gaze out your window until you do feel drowsy, and then go back to bed. Until your body is ready for sleep, tossing and turning in bed will not work.

5. If you awaken in the middle of the night, but do not have to get up, stay in bed. Give your body a chance to fall back asleep.

Even with these tips you might still have trouble getting sufficient sleep. If so, it might be helpful to consult your doctor to see if there is a medical explanation. You could also see a sleep expert for more advice, or perhaps visit a counselor or therapist to see if there is an underlying emotional problem that might be hindering you from sleeping.

FOR REFLECTION

Whether you are going through this material alone or with others, the following questions might be helpful as you reflect on your experience. Either way, it might be a good idea to answer these questions in your journal. If you are meeting with a group, bring your journal with you to help you remember your insights as you share your experiences.

1. Were you able to practice the discipline of sleep this week? If so, describe what you did and how you felt about it.

2. What, if anything, did you learn about God or yourself through the exercise?

two

God is Good

I remember the first time I was invited to speak at a church that uses "call and response" in their worship services. The worship leader would yell out something, and the congregation would respond by shouting something back. Sensing that I might not be used to this, the pastor introduced me to the congregation and then said, "In order to prepare our guest for how we do things here, let's engage in an antiphonal response we say every Sunday, and then let him try it so he can get his heart ready to preach."

The pastor paused, then shouted, *"God is good!"* and the congregation shouted back, *"All the time!"* and the pastor then countered, *"And all the time . . ."* and the congregation finished, *"God is good!"* Then he said, "Jim will now lead us." He pointed to the pulpit microphone where I, not used to shouting or being shouted at, squeaked out, "God is good." To spur me on the people shouted back very loudly, *"All the time!"* Filled with either the Holy Spirit or adrenaline or both, I shouted back, *"And all the time!"* at which they yelled back, *"God is good!"*

In those days it was easy for me to shout "God is good!" Up until that point my life had been characterized by success and blessing. I had no trouble telling anyone that I believed God was good, truly and utterly good. I had lots of evidence: a loving family, health, a beautiful and wonderful wife, a healthy young son, a great career. Some twelve years earlier I had become a Christian, and from that moment on God had been moving in my life in obvious ways. Saying, or even yelling, that God is good was easy and natural for me that Sunday morning. But all of that was about to change.

"WHO SINNED?"

The news was stunning and breathtaking. The doctors told my wife and me that the little girl she had been carrying for eight months had a rare chromosomal disorder that would likely cause her to die at birth. We went home completely disoriented and full of tears. The doctors were so matter-of-fact in announcing this bad news that I wanted to grab and shake them and say, "This is our daughter you're talking about, not some medical malfunction!" Up to that point in my life nothing terrible had happened to me. Now I was faced with one of life's worst problems—dealing with the coming death of a child. How does a person survive this kind of news? How do you move from painting your child's nursery to planning her funeral? How does a Christian, one who believes in the goodness of God, respond to something so tragic and heartbreaking?

It turned out the doctor's prognosis was wrong. She did have a chromosomal disorder, but not one that was immediately fatal. Our little Madeline (ironically, her name means "tower of strength") survived the birth but weighed only a few pounds, had a heart defect, was deaf and could not keep food down. The medical experts then told us she would not live more than a year or two. During that time both my wife and I felt as if we had been kicked in the stomach— repeatedly. It just would not end. One day a pastor I had known for years took me to lunch in an effort to comfort me. While I was in the middle of eating my salad he asked, "Who sinned, Jim, you or your wife?" I said, "Excuse me . . . what do you mean?" He said, "Well, one or both of you must have sinned at some point to have caused this to happen."

I began thinking about the bad things I had done in my life, wondering which one of them could have made God angry enough to give us a child born with terminal birth defects. *Could this pastor possibly be right?* I wondered. I could think of at least a half dozen fairly egregious sins, but nothing illegal or highly immoral and certainly none worth making a baby pay for it. Then I thought, *Maybe it was my wife! After all, he said one or both of us! Maybe she did something bad—what could it be?* I let my mind wander in this fashion the rest of the afternoon and sank deeper into a mixture of remorse and sadness, anger and suspicion. As my mind wandered down this path, it seemed that Madeline's birth was the sad sum of a simple cause-and-effect equation: God was balancing accounts or had some reason behind his actions. And to question or judge the rightness of God's actions would be to add even more sin.

Madeline lived for just over two years, and then her little body finally gave up the fight. Over those two years, and the year after, people said some outrageously ignorant and tactless things to us. During the viewing the night before Madeline's funeral, a woman said to my wife, "It's okay honey, you can have another child." The comments that started to bother me the most were the theological ones explaining what God was up to in all of this. "Well, I am sure the Lord had a reason for this," several people said. "I guess God just wanted her in heaven more than he wanted her here," said another. "Sometimes children are too beautiful for this earth," said yet another. The God they talked about

> Have you ever been through a situation that made you doubt God's goodness? If so, describe what happened and how you felt.

was too mean or too small. They wanted and needed to believe that there was a divine plan, but this plan painted a picture of a God who cared more for himself than he did for me. I was led by these Christian friends to believe that God was cruel, capricious and selfish.

According to his journal, George Fox (1624-1691), the founder of the Quaker movement, sat down by a creek and sensed the Holy Spirit whisper these words to him: "There is one, even Christ Jesus that can speak to thy condition." I believe that Jesus can and does speak to our condition. My "condition" was obvious. I—along with my wife—had been faithful (though imperfect) followers of Jesus, and we were faced with one of life's most painful experiences: burying our child. I have learned to ask myself this question when it comes to choosing the right narratives about God: *Is this understanding of God consistent with the God Jesus revealed?* What would Jesus say about our situation? Would he conclude, as did my pastor friend, that our daughter's condition was the result of our sin?

> Why does the author believe it is so important for our belief about God to be consistent with Jesus' belief? Do you agree?

AN ANCIENT NARRATIVE: THE ANGRY GOD

The pastor who asked the question "Who sinned?" was operating from a narrative that has been around for several millennia. Nearly all ancient religions were built on a narrative that says we have to do something in order to get the blessings of the gods, and conversely, if we anger the gods we will surely be punished. The narrative can be summed up as, *"God is an angry judge. If you do well, you will be blessed; if you sin, you will be punished."*

Not only is this narrative found in most primitive religions, it is also seemingly found in the Hebrew Bible. In Exodus 20:5 we read the following warning about idols: "You shall not bow down to them or worship them; for I the LORD your God am a jealous God, punishing children for the iniquity of parents, to the third and the fourth generation of those who reject me." The rabbis in Jesus' day taught this, and it was the dominant narrative among the people Jesus associated with. Bible scholar Raymond Brown notes, "The rabbis spoke of God giving men 'punishments of love,' i.e., chastisements which, if a person suffered them generously, would bring him long life and rewards."

"God is an angry judge. If you do well, you will be blessed; if you sin, you will be punished." Do you agree with this statement? Why or why not?

Though it has ancient Jewish roots, this narrative is also held by modern Christians. Shortly after the tragedy of 9/11, two popular Christian televangelists proclaimed that God was punishing the United States, and New York in particular, for its sinfulness. Apparently the God of Jesus was so fed up with gays, lesbians, strippers, gamblers and drug dealers that he inspired a group of non-Christians to fly planes into buildings for him.

This narrative is believed by more than a few people on the fringes of the faith; it is *the most prevalent narrative about God among Christians*. A study conducted at Baylor University concluded that this is the way most conservative Christians think about God. Approximately 37 percent of Christians believe that God is both "judgmental and highly engaged in the affairs of humans." Like a divine Judge, God is watching us closely, eager to punish us for even minor infractions.

Have you ever wondered how and when you would be punished by God for a particular sin? Or have you ever had something bad happen to you and wondered what you did to deserve it? Explain.

I have to confess that for many

years I believed in this narrative. If I did something especially good—prayed for a long time or spent a day in community service—I would wonder, *What blessing is God going to give me for my good works?* If, on the other hand, I did something bad—lied to a friend or skipped church to play golf—I would secretly speculate when and how God was going to punish me. It was not until I was faced with the situation of dealing with my daughter's congenital illness that I confronted this narrative. Surely our little Maddie had not sinned and caused this disease? And what possible sin could my wife or I have done that God would force a small child to suffer for it? Our situation drove me to look deeply into what I really thought about God. I went straight to the best God storyteller I could find. I turned my attention to Jesus.

JESUS' NARRATIVE

Jesus boldly proclaimed that his heavenly Father is good—good like no other: "There is only one who is good" (Matthew 19:17). In all of his stories, Jesus describes a God who seems altogether good and is always out for our good, even if we cannot understand it. And what about the narrative that says God punishes bad people? Jesus was asked about this on two occasions. The first came when he was asked to explain two horrific events, one caused by human cruelty and one caused by a natural disaster.

> At that very time there were some present who told him about the Galileans whose blood Pilate had mingled with their sacrifices. He asked them, "Do you think that because these Galileans suffered in this way they were worse sinners than all other Galileans? No, I tell you; but unless you repent, you will all perish as they did. Or those eighteen who were killed when the tower of Siloam fell on them—do you think that they were worse offenders than all the others living in Jerusalem? No, I tell you; but unless you repent, you will all perish just as they did." (Luke 13:1-5)

You can hear the "punishing God" narrative in the question, Did they suffer because they were worse sinners? Jesus unequivocally says no. He shuts down this way of thinking. If there were any correlation between sin and punishment, he could have easily said yes. He used the tragedy not to explain how God punishes people but to remind them that there is a fate worse than death.

"RABBI, WHO SINNED?"

The second time Jesus confronts the "God punishes sinners" narrative hits close to home for me. Jesus encounters a man who was born blind, and is asked a question by his disciples: " 'Rabbi, who sinned, this man or his parents, that he was born blind?' Jesus answered, 'Neither this man nor his parents sinned; he was born blind so that God's works might be revealed in him' " (John 9:2-3).

The rabbis in Jesus' day taught that illnesses were caused by the sins of the parents or of the person who was suffering. Because this man's blindness is congenital— he was *born* blind—they would assume that the blindness was caused by the parents. But some rabbis taught that a child could actually sin in the womb, so perhaps the man was at fault after all. Other ancient peoples who believed in reincarnation held that a sin in a previous life was the reason for congenital illness. Blindness, it was believed, was caused because the person had killed his mother in their previous life.

> When confronted with someone's suffering, have you ever wondered, *What did they do to deserve that?* Why is this response so common? ———>

So how did Jesus respond? Did he affirm the passage in Exodus 20:5 and say that the blindness was caused by the man's parents? Did he endorse the rabbinic position that perhaps this man committed a sin in the womb? Or did Jesus step outside of the typical Jewish nar-

Because some things are so awful that people cannot / imagine they would have happened w/o an explanation

rative and say that the blind man must have done something bad in
a previous life?

Jesus was given an opportunity to affirm the dominant narrative,
but he refuses to affirm it. His statement that "neither this man nor
his parents sinned" seems odd at first because I know no one who
has never sinned. But that is not what Jesus means by this statement;
he is making it clear that there is no correlation between someone's
sin and his or her infirmity. He could have said, "Yes, it was his parents' fault. They ran after other gods, and my Father is taking it out
on their child." He could also have said, "It was his own fault. When
he was in his mother's womb he had some covetous thoughts, and so
God made him blind." Let me emphasize again: Jesus did not say
anything like this.

What is more, Jesus heals the man of his blindness. The implications of this are far-reaching. If Jesus believed the man's blindness
was a fair and just punishment for his sins (or his parents' sins), he
would have walked away. Justice would have demanded it. Instead,
Jesus healed the blind man, and so revealed the power of God. New
Testament scholar Merrill Tenney concludes:

> Jesus refused to accept either alternative suggested by the dis-
> ciples' question. He looked on the man's plight, not as retribu-
> tion for some offense committed either by his parents or him-
> self, but as an opportunity to do God's work. Jesus did not
> consider the blindness as punishment or a matter of irrational
> chance; it was a challenge to manifest God's healing power in
> the man's life.

IT RAINS ON THE RIGHTEOUS, TOO

Jesus clearly abolished the notion that we "get what we deserve." According to Jesus, God is not in the business of balancing some eternal checkbook. In another place Jesus uses a famous phrase to show
that God treats all people the same: "He makes his sun rise on the

evil and on the good, and sends rain on the righteous and on the unrighteous" (Matthew 5:45).

Jesus is telling us an obvious truth: just as sunshine and rain are given equally to saints and sinners with no distinction, so God gives blessings to all without regard to their behavior. Terrible things happen to wonderful people. Wonderful things happen to awful people. We cannot look around the world we live in and build a case that sinners are punished and righteous people are blessed. Reality simply does not bear this out.

THERE IS NO JUSTICE IN THIS LIFE

I think I know why the narrative of the "punishing-blessing god" is so prevalent and popular. We like control. This narrative allows us to live in the illusion that we can control our world, which is very appealing in our chaotic existence. This, though, is a form of superstition—don't walk under a ladder, break a mirror or let a black cat cross your path. We know deep down that superstitions are silly, but that does not prevent us from believing in them.

The belief that God punishes and blesses us for our actions is not only superstitious, there is no evidence to support it. Augustine of Hippo, living in the fourth century, points out an obvious problem. He wrote:

> We do not know why God's judgment makes a good man poor, and a wicked man rich. . . . Nor why the wicked man enjoys the best of health, whilst the man of religion wastes away in illness. . . . Even then it is not consistent. . . . Good men also have good fortune and evil men find evil fortunes. . . . So though we do not know by what judgment these things are carried out or permitted by God, in whom is the highest virtue and the highest wisdom and the highest justice, and in whom there is no weakness nor rashness nor unfairness, it is none the less beneficial for us to learn not to regard as impor-

tant the good or evil fortunes which we see shared by good and evil persons alike.

I love Augustine's honesty—we do not know why God allows this to happen. And he also points out that good things *do* happen to the good, and bad things also happen to those who are bad.

Take infertility, for example. I know some really fine, faithful couples who cannot conceive a child, and it brings them pain and shame.

Name some of the "peculiarly good" consequences (character, disposition, reputation) that are a part of the lives of those who do good.

Today I read in my local newspaper about a mother who prostituted her little girl for drug money. Why was that woman blessed with the ability to conceive, while my friends were not? So should we conclude that good people always suffer and bad people never do? Of course not. Bad people also suffer, and good people prosper. Clearly there is no way to make sense of it all, no system to explain the whys. *Peace, Joy, contentment, communion with God, Security of eternal life*

THE GOOD ONLY THE GOOD KNOW

Even so, Augustine still continues to believe that God possesses the "highest virtue and . . . wisdom and . . . justice," and that God is neither weak nor rash nor unfair. He concludes by saying that it is not "beneficial" to spend our time worrying about why good or bad things happen. It is not worthwhile because we simply cannot know. And more importantly, it will keep us from focusing on the right things. Augustine concludes, "Rather we must seek out the good things peculiar to the good, and give the widest berth to the evils peculiar to evil men."

We should focus our attention on "the good things peculiar to the good." What does that mean? It refers to the blessings that are given only to those who strive to do good. That is the only justice, in a sense, we can count on. — *in This earthly life*

For example, as I am writing this I am in Brazil working with two pastors. For years both have been serving, preaching to and offering love to the people in Rio de Janeiro and Campinas. Though I do not speak fluent Portuguese and cannot understand what people are saying to them, I have watched throughout the day as dozens of men and women who have been blessed by their ministries come forward to hug and thank them. Pastor Eduardo's and Pastor Ricardo's faces radiated with joy.

This is something unknown to those who do wrong. Those who are selfish and spiteful and mean will never know the feeling those two pastors know. It is something peculiar to those who do good.

Conversely, Augustine says that we should also "give the widest berth to the evils peculiar to evil men." Those who are selfish and spiteful and mean are intimately acquainted with guilt, loneliness, remorse and self-hatred. They know what it feels like to have darkness surround and overtake them. This does not solve the problem entirely, but it gives us a glimpse into the goodness of God. God promises that those who love and serve, and are honest and faithful, will know a kind of joy and peace that those who are evil never will.

STILL, GOD IS JUST

We never know, in this life, why anything happens to any of us. If we are honest and objective we will have to admit that there is little justice in this life. Augustine offers one last word of wisdom about suffering. He tells us that one day we *will* understand:

> When we come to Judgment Day not only will the judgments passed there seem to be most just, but all the judgments of God from the beginning will be likewise clearly fair. Then too it will also become clear how just the judgment of God is in causing so many—in fact, almost all—of his judgments to evade men's

In one Way, it appeals to our sense of fairness
In Another, we are frustrated because we see
unfairness all around us Now.

48   THE GOOD AND BEAUTIFUL GOD

> Does the fact that God has the final say in all of life offer you comfort? Hope? Frustration? Why?

grasp of understanding. Those who have faith will not fail to realize that such hidden judgments are just.

If Augustine were my pastor he would say, "We cannot know these things here and now—they are beyond our grasp. But I believe that one day it will all become clear. One day you will fully understand why God allowed your daughter to be born with a birth defect and why she died young, and I believe that when you understand why, you will see that God was not only just, but good."

JESUS BELIEVES WHEN I CANNOT

I want to state clearly that it is not just the narratives of Jesus that have helped me, but Jesus himself has carried me along through my grief and doubt. Jesus not only *explains* suffering, he *experienced* suffering. He endured the worst kind of alienation possible as he hung on the cross, feeling that his Father had forsaken him. When we received the news about our daughter Madeline's condition, I too felt forsaken by God. Jesus understands.

In his letter to the Galatians Paul wrote this moving narrative: "I have been crucified with Christ; and it is no longer I who live, but it is Christ who lives in me. And the life I now live in the flesh I live by faith in the Son of God, who loved me and gave himself for me" (Galatians 2:19-20).

If you look closely at your Bible when you read this verse, you will probably notice a footnote after the phrase "faith in the Son of God." The footnote in most modern translations reads, "or can be translated 'the faith of the Son of God.' " This is because it seems to be a more accurate translation, and your Bible translators want to be honest. So why do most translations not read that way? I think it is because we tend to emphasize our faith in Jesus, and are not used to thinking about Jesus' faith for us.

Jesus said his Father was good. Jesus also refused to affirm the idea that external rewards and punishments are given by God on the basis of our good or bad works. Rain falls on the good and the bad. Sometimes we pray for rain (for our crops), and sometimes we pray that it will not rain (for our picnics). Both good and bad people get rained on, whether they want it or not. Jesus faced suffering, rejection and alienation, and the people jeered at him as he hung on the cross, questioning whether God was really with him. And Jesus believed. And he believes for me. He believes even when we cannot. He prays even when we cannot. We participate in *his* faith.

I affirm with Paul that I have been crucified with Christ. I do not understand that mystery, but I know that Jesus is closer to me than I am to myself. Christ lives in me, and I live by his faith. I am not alone. This is something more than simply getting my narratives right. It is allowing Jesus to live in and through and for me. The love of the Father, the redemption of Jesus and the communion I have with the Spirit are not based on anything I do. It is a gift from the Holy Spirit to believe in a God who is good even when things look bleak.

A REASON FOR HOPE

A few years after Madeline died I was in the middle of a day of solitude. My mind went over the last few years, thinking about the pain of hearing the news from the doctors, the countless sleepless nights on hospital floors, and the dark and rainy day we placed her body in the earth. I turned to God and said, without thinking, "Maybe it would have been better if she had never been born."

That was when I received one of the clearest experiences of God responding to me that I've ever had in my life. On this day, at that moment, a little voice penetrated my mind, the voice of a little girl, a voice I had never heard but immediately recognized as Madeline's. "Daddy, you should never say that. If I had never been born, I would not be here now. I am so happy here in heaven, and one day you and Mom and Jacob will come and see me, and we will live forever together. And there is more good that has happened because of me that you can't see now but will one day understand."

I immediately repented of my despicable thoughts and crumpled to the ground in tears. I was thankful to hear such words. Another narrative had entered my mind—the story about the promise of heaven. I was beginning to see how a person could face tragedy and still say "God is good to me," to understand how Job could say, "Though he slay me, yet will I trust in him" (Job 13:15 KJV), and to know how Jesus could tremble in a garden and still call his Father "Abba."

Two years after Madeline's death my wife, Meghan, became pregnant. For eight months we lived with a lot of anxiety, mixed with a little faith. When it came time to have that final sonogram, our hearts were in our throats, bracing for bad news. The technician, who did not know our story, kept saying things we loved to hear: "Perfect hands . . . perfect heart . . . your baby looks just perfect. Do you want to know the gender?" We said yes. "It's a little girl." We both smiled. "What are you going to name her?" she asked.

At the very same moment we said, "Hope."

IN THIS WORLD YOU WILL HAVE TROUBLE

It has now been a decade since Madeline died. So much now seems clear to me in regard to the nature of God. God's goodness is not something I get to decide upon. I am a human being with limited understanding, and as I grow and mature in my walk of faith I increasingly see how little I understand. In the end, I have the testimony of Jesus to stand on. My own experiences of disappointment with God say more about me and my expectations than they do about God. The goodness of God, I now see with greater clarity, is vast and consuming. Jesus never promises that our lives will be free of struggle. In fact, he said quite the opposite: "In the world ye shall have tribulation: but be of good cheer; I have overcome the world" (John 16:33 KJV).

We should expect to go through heartache and pain, suffering and loss, because they are part of what it means to be human, and they can be useful in our development. As James said, "My brothers and sisters, whenever you face trials of any kind, consider it nothing but joy, because you know that the testing of your faith produces endurance; and let endurance have its full effect, so that you may be mature and complete, lacking in nothing" (James 1:2-4).

I have grown much more through my trials than I have through my successes. I do not ask for trials, and I am not as deep in God's kingdom as was James, so I don't consider trials "nothing but joy," but I am learning to trust God in the midst of them.

To be sure, I have been through a lot of trials over the past few years. I have not been asked back to preach at the "call and response" church, but I do not need a pulpit to proclaim that God is good. I know with certainty that God did not punish my daughter with a congenital illness because of the sins of my wife, me or my daughter. And I know that God is just. And I also hold fast to the hope of heaven, a place where wrongs are made right and where I will understand fully. I believe all of this because of the faith of the Son of God who loved me and gave himself for me. No matter where I am I can say with confidence, "God is good all the time, and all the time *God is good!*"

silence And Awareness of creation

What can we do to help us know and experience the goodness of God? What kind of practices can we do to help us become aware of the God Jesus knows? There are two exercises that will help us begin to experience the goodness of God. The first involves slowing down, becoming quiet and learning to be present in the present moment. The second entails paying attention to the beauty that surrounds us.

SILENCE

Our world is noisy and hurried, and few of us stop to be still. The God who is good can only reach us when we are quiet. To paraphrase the psalmist, we must be "still" to know that God is "good." This week I encourage you to try to find five minutes each day to sit in silence. Get a cup of something warm and delicious, find a comfortable chair, and just sit quietly. That's all. It is not terribly difficult, but it yields great benefits. Some tips:

- Look for little free spaces in your day, such as a break between activities.

- Get up a little earlier or leave for your next appointment a little sooner so that when you arrive you will have extra time to find a quiet place and "just be."

- A lot of people find that their thoughts run to and fro during this time of silence. This is normal. Your mind is used to helping you solve problems; it is not used to being still. Here are two tips that will help with the crazy "thought monkeys" that plague the discipline of silence:

1. Have a notepad nearby to jot down things that may come to your mind, such as a phone call you need to make or the laundry that needs to be done. This will help quiet your mind.

2. You may want to "ease in" to the five minutes by reading the Bible for a minute or two.

It may seem challenging at first, but with a little effort you should be able to do this easily every day. I suspect that soon you will find this exercise increasingly important to your daily life. It will help you slow down and become present, more able to focus on God in your midst. It might lead you into a regular practice of developing "rests" that make the notes (your actions) in your life become beautiful music.

AWARENESS OF CREATION

Historically, great theologians have cited the created world and its beauty as the first sign of God's goodness. Paul said as much in the opening chapter of his epistle to the Romans. Creation speaks of the goodness and glory of God through dazzling colors and intoxicating scents. The sunrises and sunsets are grand spectacles that happen twice each day and are seldom noticed by people too busy to look. God could have made an ugly world; he was not obligated to make a world that inspires awe. Beauty has a lot to do with order. Simply gazing at a daisy reveals the mind of God.

In her book *Experiencing God's Tremendous Love,* Maureen Conroy advises us to "become deeply absorbed in creation" as a way of experiencing God's goodness and love. She advocates this exercise experience: take a walk outside and pay great attention to the sights, sounds and colors of nature. If you have access, go to a park or some place that is relatively untouched by humans. Take something to write on and act as if you are on a mission to canvass a small area, jotting down everything you see. Pretend you're trying to communicate what you are seeing to someone who has never been able to go outdoors and experience the beauty of the created world. Note the color of the birds, the symmetry of the leaves and the sounds of the wind. Think of God as a great artist and yourself as the art student, paying close attention to the detail of the artwork.

FOR REFLECTION

Whether you are going through this material alone or with others, the following questions might be helpful as you reflect on your experience. Either way, it might be a good idea to answer these questions in your journal. If you are meeting with a group, bring your journal with you to help you remember your insights as you share your experiences.

1. Were you able to practice any of the exercises this week? If so, describe what you did and how you felt about it.

2. What, if anything, did you learn about God or yourself through the exercises?

3. Was it hard for you to find five minutes for silence each day?

4. What stood out for you as you paid closer attention to the created world around you?

three

god is trustworthy

When my son, Jacob, was six years old, I took him to an amusement park. There were only a few people in the park that day, so we went from ride to ride without having to wait. We came upon a ride that I had never ridden before but I assumed was fun. After all, we were in an *amusement* park. We got in our seats and a teenaged boy buckled us in. Soon the ride started whirling and spinning us, faster and faster, jerking us around and up and down. I held on to Jacob as hard as I could, afraid that he would fly out of his seat. With white knuckles and gritted teeth I prayed the entire ninety seconds for the ride to end. I looked over at Jacob, who was laughing and having a great time.

When we got off the ride, I saw the name of it in bright red paint: The Scrambler, which was appropriate. Jacob said, "That was fun, let's do it again!" I said no. (What I felt like saying was, "Not a chance! Ever again! I am the worst father ever! Please forgive me.") We sat down on a nearby park bench, and I asked, "Weren't you scared? That ride was pretty wild. Why did you get on a ride like that?" He answered with childlike honesty, "Because you did, Dad." Right or wrong, that little guy trusted me. I was and am clearly not worthy of such trust. I love him and would do anything for him, and I would never put him in harm's way intentionally. But I am a limited, finite, ignorant human being. In his eyes, however, being with me meant he was completely safe.

That illustrated for me why it is so essential that we understand that God is trustworthy. The God Jesus reveals would never do anything to harm us. He has no malice or evil intentions. He is completely good. And the fact that God is also all-knowing and all-powerful makes his goodness even better. I can trust God, even if things look bleak. It does not matter that God is all-powerful or all-knowing if he is not *all-good*. If he isn't all-good, I will never be able to love and trust him.

> How would you describe your trust level when it comes to God? Have things happened to you that made you doubt that God is trustworthy?

FALSE NARRATIVES

Not everyone believes that God is trustworthy. One afternoon I received a phone call from a young man who sounded as if he could not breathe. At first I thought he had just witnessed or been involved in a tragic accident. I was not well acquainted with him; he had heard me speak at a conference a few months before and found my teaching to be contrary to his own beliefs (our narratives collided). He called because he could not start his car. There was nothing wrong with the car; *he* was the problem.

"Dr. Smith, I need to know if what you said about God is true."

"What, specifically, are you referring to?"

"You said that God is entirely good and loving and trustworthy and out for our good. I wrote down every word you said. Are you sure I can trust God?"

"Yes. I am certain. Why do you ask?"

"I haven't been able to drive my car for the past few days."

"Why?" I asked.

"Because I'm afraid that I might have some bad or evil or lustful thought in my head, and in the next instant I might die in a car crash. I'm sure that God will send me straight to hell because I won't have time to repent."

After we talked for a while, I probed to find out what kinds of stories he had heard about God while growing up. He told me that from the time he was a young boy, he heard his pastor—a man who represented God and spoke on God's behalf—begging people, week after week, to stop sinning before it was too late. And if they did sin, they had better be sure to repent before it was too late. God hates sin so much that he would send a person—even a baptized believer—into everlasting punishment for committing a single sin. This narrative of the nature of God that had filled the young man's mind from an early age was ruining his life. *intentional*

I invited him to tell his story. The god of his narrative was not worthy of trust. To trust someone is to believe that he or she has your best interests in mind, that the person will protect you from harm and is reliable. This was not true of the god the young man had been exposed to. Instead of inspiring confidence and courage, his god made him afraid to drive his car. In the process of relating this narrative, he realized that the narrative he had accepted was not necessarily the truth about God. *Christians still are harmed in many instances — even if they TRUST God.*

JESUS' CORE NARRATIVES *(MARTYRS, Missionaries, crime victims)*

I encouraged this young man to compare his narrative of God with the God Jesus knows. Jesus said, "All things have been handed over to me by my Father; and no one knows who the Son is except the Father, or who the Father is except the Son and anyone to whom the Son chooses to reveal him" (Luke 10:22). Jesus revealed an enormous amount of information about his heavenly Father through a single word: *Abba*.

God as Abba. In the garden of Gethsemane, during his final hours before the crucifixion, Jesus addressed God using a unique title: Abba. This is key because Jesus' use of this title reveals something important about the nature of the God he knew. *Abba* is best translated "Dear Father." It is a term of intimacy, but it also contains a sense of obedience. The fact that Jesus addressed God with the word *Abba* tells us that, to him, God was not distant or far removed, but was intimately involved in his life. It does not in itself tell us that God is good (neither *dear* nor *father* necessarily means *good*), but as New Testament scholar C. F. D. Moule notes, "The intimate word conveys not a casual sort of familiarity but the deepest, most trustful reverence."

Jesus uses this title in his address to God while facing the most difficult hour of his life. He prays, "Abba, Father, for you all things are possible; remove this cup from me; yet, not what I want, but what you want" (Mark 14:36). Jesus is facing torture and death. In the Gospel of Luke we are told that he was in so much anguish his sweat became like drops of blood (Luke 22:44). Yet he prays, "not what I want, but what you want." How can he speak to God in this way at such a difficult moment? The only answer I can see is that he trusts his Father.

> What does Jesus' use of the word *Abba* tell us about his relationship with God the Father?

God is a good and loving Father, Jesus is telling us, and he is so good that we can obey him no matter what. But some people may ask, Why did Jesus doubt at all? He was God, after all! True, he was God, but he was also fully human. Incarnation (becoming human) implies limitation. Because he was fully human, Jesus experienced everything we do, which includes fear and doubt. But notice: even in the midst of doubt, in the moment of his deepest suffering, Jesus trusted in his heavenly Father.

God as Father. Jesus not only addressed God as Abba but also as

Father. This has raised questions for some people: Does this mean that God is male? And what about people who have a bad, abusive or absent earthly father? What if they have a hard time addressing God as Father? And how can God be a father to Jesus? Did Jesus also have a mother?

At the end of a day of teaching on prayer, I closed the meeting with a prayer that began, "Dear heavenly Father . . ." A woman came up to me afterward, full of tears, and said, "I loved all that you taught us today about prayer, but when you started your prayer by calling God 'Father' you lost me. I had a terrible father, and I cannot think of God as my Father." While I felt badly for this woman, not using the word *Father* is not the solution. The problem is that we begin with our understanding of what *father* means and then project that onto God.

That is not how it ought to work. When Jesus describes God as his Father, we have to *let him define what fatherhood means*. Karl Barth is helpful here: "It is . . . not that there is first of all human fatherhood and then a so-called divine fatherhood, but just the reverse; true and proper fatherhood resides in God and from this fatherhood what we know as fatherhood among us men is derived."

How would you respond to a person who says, "I have trouble calling God 'Father' because my biological father was not very good"?

What does Barth mean? The Trinity existed before the world was created. Long before God made humankind "in his image, . . . male and female," God existed as Father, Son and Spirit. The relationship between Jesus and God has been defined—by Jesus—as that of Father and Son. Their relationship existed before any human male had offspring. God as Father and Jesus as Son existed before any human father and son (or daughter) existed.

Therefore, fatherhood is first defined by God and Jesus, not by

Adam and his children. This has tremendous implications—and a
great deal of healing—for us. Many people, like the woman I mentioned previously, have been deeply wounded by their biological fathers, and this makes thinking about God as Father very difficult.
The solution is not to abandon the term *father* but to let Jesus define
it. Though Jesus tells a few parables in which there is a father (nota-
bly, the parable of the prodigal son), I think it is better to look at how
Jesus prayed to his Father to understand what his Father is like.

OUR FATHER

Jesus reveals the *nature* of the God to whom he prays in the *content*
of his prayer. His disciples asked him to teach them how to pray,
presumably because Jesus' prayer life was vibrant and passionate.
Jesus responded to the request by teaching them a prayer that is familiar to many:

> Pray then in this way:
> Our Father in heaven,
> hallowed be your name.
> Your kingdom come.
> Your will be done,
>   on earth as it is in heaven.
> Give us this day our daily bread.
> And forgive us our debts,
>   as we also have forgiven our debtors.
> And do not bring us to the time of trial,
>   but rescue us from the evil one. (Matthew 6:9-13)

He tells us to begin our prayer by addressing God as "Father,"
which is what he did, but note this: *the fatherhood of God is defined by
his prayer.* What do we learn from his prayer?

First, we learn that God is near: "Our Father in heaven." In Jewish
cosmology heaven did not refer to a place that is far away; heaven
referred to the surrounding atmosphere, the very air they breathed.

(Remember at Jesus' baptism when "heaven" was opened? It was not far away!) In short, God is *present.*

Second, we learn that God is holy: "hallowed be your name." Holiness has to do with purity. Jesus is teaching us that there is nothing bad about God. God can neither sin nor participate in evil. In one word, God is *pure.*

Third, we also learn that God is the King who rules heaven: "Your kingdom come. Your will be done, on earth as it is in heaven." Kings have power over others, and God is "the King of kings." In short, God is *powerful.*

So far we are not told anything that would lead us to believe that God is looking out for our good. People have believed in many gods who are in their midst, who are holy and powerful yet not necessarily caring. It is in the next few petitions that we discover the compassionate nature of the God of Jesus.

Fourth, we learn that God is one who cares for us: "Give us . . . our daily bread." We have a God who makes rain and sunshine and a great bounty of food for all of his creatures—even the birds of the air. Thus we learn that God *provides.*

Fifth, God is one who forgives our trespasses. As Richard Foster notes, "At the heart of God is the desire to forgive and to give." God loves to forgive, even more than we long to be forgiven. In a word, our Father *pardons.*

Sixth, we learn from the Lord's Prayer that God rescues us from trials and evils—"do not bring us to the time of trial, but rescue us from the evil one." God is present and powerful because he longs to *protect* us. Though we will suffer problems, accidents or trials, God gets the last word. Nothing can happen to us that God cannot redeem.

Jesus' Father is nearby, holy, powerful, caring, forgiving and our protector. These attributes provide strong images of who God is and what fatherhood means. And we now have a way to define the Father's goodness. We also have a way to measure what true parenthood ought to be. A good parent, be it a father or mother, ought to possess these six characteristics.

As a father, I try hard, but often fail, to reflect each of those six characteristics. I am near to my children, but sometimes I am distant, preferring to read the newspaper than play with them. And my work sometimes takes me far away for weeks at a time. I also try hard to be good and pure, but I fail miserably at times, snapping at them for minor infractions and being petty and selfish. I try to be strong for my kids, but sometimes I am scared and confused, just as they are. I do a decent job of providing for them, but sometimes I provide too much and spoil them. I forgive them, but I catch myself bringing up their past mistakes. And I try to protect them, but I am woefully aware that I cannot protect them from all enemies that lurk about. My children, my wife and most of my friends would rate me as a decent father. Every Father's Day both of my children write me cards and say, "You are the best dad ever." But I am aware of my deficiencies and pray that my children do not suffer because of them.

> Of the six aspects of the nature of God the Father (present, pure, powerful, provides, pardons, protects) as seen in the Lord's Prayer, which do you most need to see and understand about God?

My point here is that God's fatherhood must define what human fatherhood ought to look like, and not the reverse. The "How to Be a Good Dad" booklet I keep on my bedside table has some nice tips ("Play with your kids" and "Listen to them"), but I would do a lot better drawing near to my heavenly Father and allowing him to shape my heart into his image. The way God is Father to me teaches me how to be a good father to my children.

The woman who could not pray to God as Father had a horrific childhood, marked by an abusive and distant father. When she projects her idea of a father onto God, she sees someone she could never love or trust. Telling her to just "get over it because Jesus called God Father and so must you" would be cruel. The better solution is to encourage her to let Jesus define what *Father* means and thereby come to know the God Jesus knows. In doing so, she might find healing.

The God that Jesus reveals is not only a perfect reflection of what fatherhood ought to be but motherhood as well. Sometimes we think of fathers as strong and stern providers, and mothers as gentle and meek supporters. But in Jesus' description of the Father we see a perfect balance of all of these characteristics. A good mother would be one who is near, whole, strong, giving, forgiving and protecting. In fact, a good *person*, male or female, single or married, with or without children, possesses these characteristics. Jesus is also a reflection of the Father, so when we see him we see God the Father. In Jesus we see a perfect balance of all of the characteristics of goodness. Jesus is indeed gentle, but he is also strong when needed.

FINDING OUR TRUE FATHER

I met a pastor from England whose own story beautifully illustrates what it means to trust God as our Father. I asked Carl how he came to be a Christian. He said that when he was growing up he seldom went to church. He was very close with his dad, though. When he was fourteen, his father died in a tragic accident at work, which completely shattered Carl's life. To numb his pain, he started getting into a lot of fights at school and soon was abusing alcohol. But nothing seemed to work.

When Carl was seventeen a friend invited him to what Carl thought was a party, complete with binge drinking, so he agreed. It was actually a "Christian house party," which is common in England and is more like a retreat. People go to a big home and hang out for a few days of conversation, worship and recreation. When he found out, it was too late to turn back. After the first two days he still felt bitter toward God. But during a time of worship on the final day, Sunday morning, he heard a distinct voice that said, "I am your Father. Come to me." Carl said he immediately began to sob, and for the first time since his father died his heart began to heal.

All of us have to face pain and difficulty, sometimes even tragedy. As we come to know and draw close to the God Jesus knows, we find a new kind of strength to deal with our struggles. If we do not know God as our Abba Father, then we will never have the courage to face our problems. But as we come to know the good and beautiful God that Jesus knows, our struggles take on a whole new meaning. If God is truly good and is looking out for our good, then we can come to him with complete honesty. We can practice honesty when we pray— baring our soul and confronting those hurts that make us doubt God's goodness by handing them over to him for healing.

WHAT IS YOUR CUP?

Earlier in this chapter I mentioned how Jesus faced a difficult situation in the garden of Gethsemane. He asked his Abba to remove his "cup" from him. The cup represents the things that are forced on us in life. We all must ask, *What is my "cup"?* What aspect of your life makes it difficult for you to trust God? Were you hurt by a divorce? Have you suffered loss? Are you unable to find a life partner and struggling with the prospect of lifelong singleness? Have you experienced the death of a loved one? The death of a dream? The loss of a business? The loss of some physical capacity?

> What is your "cup"? How have you dealt with it? What did you learn about God or yourself through that experience?

A "cup" is anything that we struggle with accepting as our lot in life. And our cup is usually the thing that makes it difficult to believe God is good. Being told by our doctors that our daughter would be born with terminal birth defects was the first of many cups for me. Like Jesus, I faced something that conflicted with own desires. I wanted a healthy daughter. Would I be able to say, "Abba, Father" when I prayed?

Some years later I read Thomas Smail's interpretation of what Jesus was going through in the garden of Gethsemane, and how he was able to trust God in the midst of his pain. It helped me understand something important about trusting God, and it answered a question people asked of me: "Jim, how can you still trust God after what you went through?" For years I did not know how to answer this question, but now I do. Smail explains:

> The Father that Jesus addresses in the garden is the one that he has known all his life and found to be bountiful in his provision, reliable in his promises and utterly faithful in his love. He can obey the will that sends him to the cross, with hope and expectation because it is the will of Abba whose love has been so proved that it can now be trusted so fully by being obeyed so completely. This is not legal obedience driven by commandment, but trusting response to known love.

He states it well: our relationship to the Father is a "trusting response to known love." Jesus knew he was loved by his Father and was therefore able to trust him through the pain. The reason Jesus could trust God in his darkest hour is because he had lived closely with his good and beautiful Father for all eternity. I now see how love that has been proved can be trusted even when things don't make sense. So when I encounter a world full of tsunamis and child molesters, airplane crashes and methadone-addicted moms, I don't try to force myself to say all is well. Rather, I say, "Jesus trusted his Abba, and I will also trust in the God I know to be good."

JOINING OUR NARRATIVE WITH GOD'S NARRATIVE

The day that our daughter died came unexpectedly. She had not responded well to surgery, and her body began shutting down. Mad-

eline had done this before but always managed to recover. Still, I
came quickly to the hospital from a worship service, and fortunately
I was accompanied by my friend Father Paul Hodge, who is a priest
in the Orthodox Church in America. As Madeline lay dying, Father
Paul prayed with my wife and me. From his prayer book he chose a
prayer with ancient roots and deep theological teaching. The following is the exact prayer he prayed:

> Our thoughts are not Your thoughts O Lord, and our ways are
> not Your ways. We confess to You that we cannot see Your di-
> vine hand in the suffering of Madeline. Help us, we beg You, to
> see that in this evil there is some purpose, beyond our grasp
> and comprehension. Our minds are confused. Our hearts are in
> distress. Our wills are lost and weak, and our strength is gone,
> as we see this innocent creature caught by the sins of the world
> and the power of the devil, a victim of senseless suffering and
> pain. Have mercy on this child, Lord, have mercy! Do not pro-
> long the agony! Do not allow the pain and suffering to increase!
> We know not what to ask You; give us the grace only to say,
> "Your will be done on earth, as it is in heaven." Give us faith, for
> we believe, O Lord; help our unbelief. Be with Your child Mad-
> eline, and suffer with her; heal her and save her, according to
> Your own saving plan, established before the creation of the
> world. For You are our only hope, O God, and in You we take
> refuge: Father, Son and Holy Spirit, now and ever, and unto ages
> of ages. Amen.

Months and even years later both Meghan and I remember this
prayer vividly. It was a healing moment for us, and it prepared us for
our daughter's passing.

Why? The prayer took our story, our own personal narratives (a
mother, a father and a sick child), and put it in the context of a larger
story, a metanarrative, which is the story that God is writing. It gave
words to our anguish as well as to our hopes. The prayer is honest:

we cannot see God's "divine hand," and we want to see that there is purpose to it all. It is only when our suffering seems meaningless that our spirits are finally broken. But the prayer goes on. It states that we still believe even in our unbelief. It placed our suffering in the proper setting: God's "own saving plan, established before the creation of the world." God is good, and God is still in control, and God's kingdom is never in trouble.

When we join our story to God's, the story in which our good and beautiful God gets the last word, then everything begins to make sense. The pain is still real, but it becomes bearable. We can then, in time, begin to move on. And we can begin to see beyond the suffering and look toward the widespread mercy that surrounds us.

FOCUSING ON BLESSINGS, NOT ONLY ON CUPS

Thomas Smail said Jesus was able to trust God because he found God to be "bountiful in his provision." Jesus was keenly aware of the goodness of God because God had been with him every day, blessing him and all that he did. That is why he continued to trust God even in the final, awful moments. In order to withstand discouraging circumstances, we need to develop the clear sense that God is out for our good. We can do this by increasingly becoming aware of the blessings that attend our every moment.

George Buttrick (1892-1980) was the pastor of the Madison Avenue Presbyterian Church in New York City from 1927 until 1954. He was a powerful preacher, teacher and writer. His book *Prayer* is considered one of the best books on prayer ever written. One day I came across a passage in that book that forever changed my way of looking at the world. In it Buttrick tells the story of a man who used a unique illustration to help people see the goodness of God.

A lecturer to a group of businessmen displayed a sheet of white paper in which was one blot. He asked what they saw. All answered, "A blot." The test was unfair; it invited the wrong answer. Nevertheless, there is an ingratitude in human nature by which we notice the black disfigurement and forget the widespread mercy. We need to deliberately call to mind the joys of our journey. Perhaps we should try to write down the blessings of one day. We might begin: we could never end: there are not pens or paper enough in all the world. The attempt would remind us of our "vast treasure of content."

Buttrick is clear: we must "deliberately" call to mind the blessings that are all around us. If we had the eyes to see all of them, the pens and paper in the whole world could not write them down. He is not advocating "positive thinking"; he is telling us a deep truth about the universe we live in.

I once watched a child open her presents at a birthday party that all of her friends and their parents attended. She especially wanted a certain gift that she did not get. One by one she opened each package, and the child who gave it watched, smiling with anticipation, only to watch her snub her nose and push the package aside. It was painfully embarrassing to all of us, especially to the birthday girl's parents. It was a startling example of ingratitude. She was given gift after gift, and all she could think about was the one gift she wanted. I later learned that the gift she wanted was neither precious nor valuable, but was inferior to many of the gifts she received.

Did George Buttrick's blot illustration ring true for you? How might you begin shifting your attention away from the negative and onto the positive?

As I drove home I thought about how awful that experience was, and how spoiled and ungrateful that little girl was. Then the Spirit whispered, "Are you so different?" I thought about how often I focus on something I want God to do for me, and neglect the ten thousand things—often better things—he has already done. I fuss about my "cups," little and large (not having enough money to do this or that, a problem at work, a strain in a relationship), and never once stop and thank God that I have eyes to see. If I lost my sight and had a million dollars, I would gladly pay it to get my eyesight back. My eyes are worth a million dollars. So is my heart. And my ears. And my wife. And my children. If I were wise, I would spend time each day thanking God for the "vast treasure" he has given me. I could start, but I could never stop.

Our troubles are real. But they are small compared to God's "widespread mercy," as Buttrick said. The more we are able to see just how many blessings we have been given—given freely and undeserved—the more we will be able to see that God is out for our good. And when that happens, our trust level increases.

My son got on a scary amusement-park ride with me that he should have been frightened of, but instead he smiled the entire time. Why? *Because of who was on the ride with him.* Throughout his entire life I have taken care of him. I have fed him, clothed him, bathed him, prayed with him, taken care of him when he was sick and provided everything he ever needed. Jacob trusted me without hesitation.

You and I are in a similar situation. The life we are living is at times scary but is also a great deal of fun. The key is to *remember who is riding with us.* There is not a single situation you and I will face that we must face alone. God is with us. God is out for our good. Even in the most painful of circumstances God is able to redeem it, for "we know that all things work together for good" (Romans 8:28) for those who trust in him. The least we can do is enjoy the ride.

counting your blessings

Counting your blessings is a powerful spiritual exercise. Make a list of all of the things God has blessed you with, all of the things that make life wonderful. Pay attention to the details of your life. Look for the hidden things. Take notice of all of those wonderful things you easily overlook. Start small: try to come up with a list of ten things God has blessed you with. It can include things like your loved ones, material provision or opportunities you have been given. It can also include things in the created world: the sun, the stars, the mountains and so forth. Or you might want to include things you love, like coffee or ice cream! Finally, also include things that God has done for you. Each day God is at work providing for us, even though we cannot always see it. This exercise is aimed at helping you see "the widespread mercy" that is so much greater than the "black blot."

Keep adding to your list each day. Strive to make a list of fifty things. Then keep going! See if you can come up with one hundred blessings, things you are thankful for, this week. You will likely end up with, as George Buttrick called it, a "vast treasure." Most of us are accustomed to waking up and thinking about our problems. This exercise will help us shift our focus away from the few things that are wrong to the many things that are beautiful and wonderful.

If you are having trouble getting started, below is a list I started a few years ago, after reading a book called *10,000 Things to Praise God*

For. I love some of the praiseworthy things in the book and added some of my own. I have done this exercise with dozens of people through the years, and I have added some of theirs. My list omits my family and friends, not because I'm not thankful for them, but because I have learned to give thanks for them on a regular basis. I wanted my list to be a reminder to praise God for the things I often overlook.

JIM'S ONGOING LIST OF BLESSINGS

God's existence

God's presence with me

Jesus

the church

a glass of iced tea on a hot day

books

naps that refresh

the loved one who finally
  came to know God

tennis

colors

smells

dreams—day or night

sunshine

the wisdom of others

laughter

a stranger's smile

my dog wagging its tail,
  happy to see me

music

clean socks

the "Hallelujah Chorus"

mentors

a child's hugs

ice cream

curiosity

the smell of the woods

poetry

warm cookies

the ocean

people who are lights

the wonder of the
  immune system

coffee

the smell of rain

prayer

the hope of heaven that
  awaits me

second chances

butterflies

longtime friends

parents loving their kids

Christmas

enriching conversations

the Bible

scientists who discover
  amazing things

chocolate

encouragement	how my mind opens to new
talented people who	understandings when I travel
are humble	the silencing of false rumors
air conditioning	the great hymns
artists	

MAKING PRAISE A HABIT

I hope that this listing exercise will not be just a one-time exercise but a new, ongoing habit that turns into a lifestyle. Musician and author David Crowder writes:

> When good is found and we embrace it with abandon, we embrace the Giver of it. . . . Every second is an opportunity to praise. There is a choosing to be made. A choosing at each moment. This is the Praise Habit. Finding God moment by revelatory moment, in the sacred and the mundane, in the valley and on the hill, in triumph and tragedy, and living praise erupting because of it. That is what we were made for.

I believe he is right. When we are grateful for something as ordinary as "curiosity," we are offering praise to God. In every single moment we have an opportunity to find something worth being amazed by. The more we do it, the more likely it will become a habit, and eventually we will find ourselves doing it without thinking. We will become, as Augustine said, "An Alleluia from head to toe."

FOR REFLECTION

Whether you are going through this material alone or with others, the following questions might be helpful as you reflect on your experience. Either way, it might be a good idea to answer these questions in your journal. If you are meeting with a group, bring your journal with you to help you remember your insights as you share your experiences.

1. Were you able to make a list of your blessings this week? If so, did you find it difficult? Why?

2. What, if anything, did you learn about God or yourself through the exercise?

3. What were some of the things that made your list that surprised you? Why?

four

God is Generous

Dallas Willard writes: "The process of spiritual formation in Christ is one of progressively replacing . . . destructive images and ideas with the images and ideas that filled the mind of Jesus himself. . . . Spiritual formation in Christ moves toward a total interchange of *our* ideas and images for *his*."

During my junior year of college, word spread to our campus about a woman who was preaching "fire and brimstone" sermons each day at a nearby university. I was a religion major and hoped one day to be a pastor, so I was intrigued by all of the fuss this woman was causing. Students were gathering by the hundreds to hear her—not because they were moved by her messages but to mock her. They called her "the little lady prophet," and precisely at 10:50 every weekday morning she would stand up on a park bench in the middle of the campus and start preaching—rebuking, really—for about twenty minutes. Each week the crowds got larger and larger. I had to see what this was all about.

I arrived about ten minutes before her starting time. Lots of students congregated in the courtyard near the famous bench. Right on time this short, plain-looking woman in an old-fashioned off-white dress—looking as if she had just emerged from an 1890s photo—strutted to the bench. She stood up on her "pulpit," looked down and, with her back to the crowd, appeared to be praying. The moment she turned around the crowd began cheering (or was it a jeering)? She raised her hands to quiet them and then, with her tattered King James Bible thrust into the air, began her sermon (or was it a tongue-lashing)?

"The eyes of the Lord are upon all of you sinners! Do not think God does not see all that you do. He brought me to this campus because he is sick of all of your wicked ways. He knows about all of the fornicating, all of the drunkenness, all of the lying and cheating, and he has one word for all of you sinners—you are all going to be thrown into the . . ." and the crowd shouted along with her, *"lake of fire!"* She was neither encouraged nor amused by the students mocking and mimicking; she went on undeterred. She got more specific with the naming of sins, and at the end of each litany they all shouted with her, "and you are all going to be thrown into the *lake of fire!"*

> What are some of the "destructive images and ideas" you have wrestled with?

I leaned up against the cold wall of the student center and watched this surreal drama unfold. As a Christian I believe that every single sin she named is a sin. Contrary to the other students around me, who cavalierly mocked her and her message, I knew that part of what she was saying was true. The little prophet lady had a clear narrative: God is mad at you because of your sin, and your sin is going to cause you to burn forever in hell. But she never mentioned God's love. There was no reference to God's grace. Jesus' name was never uttered in the entire half-hour. She spoke against sin, but only in regard to the punishment it incurs, not the damage it causes to one's soul. In addition to an incomplete narrative, she added nothing that might help a person change, other than guilt and fear, which are not effective, lasting motivations.

Where did this woman get this narrative about God? And what would Jesus say to the little lady prophet?

FALSE NARRATIVE: EARNING FAVOR

Though her narrative is extreme, it is not uncommon. It is not often uttered in such stark language, so black and white, or so simply. Her dominant narrative is of earning God's favor, and it is a deeply imbedded narrative in our culture and many of our churches. This narrative goes like this: Love and forgiveness are commodities that are exchanged for performance. God's love, acceptance and forgiveness must be merited by right living. What God most wants is for us not to sin and instead to do good. This narrative is rooted, as all false narratives are, in a half-truth. True, God does not want us to sin, and God does want us to do well. But that is only because sin harms us, and acts of goodness are healing both to us and to the recipients of our goodness.

The cultural narrative of earning. This narrative is rooted in our world, where earning is the means by which we obtain things. From a young age we learn that our parents' love is dependent on our good behavior; that school grades are given based on our performance; that affection is offered on attractiveness; that rejection, loneliness and isolation are the consequences

> How does our culture support the narrative of earning? Have you felt this pressure?

of failure. When every person in every situation in every day of our lives treats us on the basis of how we look, act and perform, it is difficult not to project that onto God. After all, God is bigger than our parents, more aware than our authority figures and sees more of us than our closest friends do.

Therefore the all-seeing, all-knowing God is aware of every bad thing we have ever thought or done. If God were our parent, he would withhold his love, just as our parents did when we behaved badly ("Go to your room! No dinner for you"). If God were our teacher, we would get an F ("This was a poor effort"). If God were our judge, the verdict would be "Guilty as charged." Guilt, fear, shame and the hunger for acceptance become the primary motivators in our performance-based culture.

The (misunderstood) biblical narrative of earning. Not only our world and our culture, but also the Bible itself is used to support the earning-favor narrative. The Israelites are punished and sent into exile by Yahweh for their disobedience. David's illegitimate child dies, presumably because it was conceived in an act of adultery. Yet there is a larger narrative that should guide our understanding of these stories. The Israelites were chosen by Yahweh for no apparent reason and were delivered from bondage and into a land of milk and honey despite having done nothing to deserve it. David's act of adultery and murder should have resulted in his own death, but instead he becomes a man "after God's own heart." David has another son, Solomon, by the same woman with whom he committed adultery, and Solomon becomes wise, powerful and wealthy. To say that sin has consequences is different than saying that because of our sin God entirely rejects us.

Even though we can find a few "narratives of earning" from select Bible passages, there is only enough cloth to make a small quilt of guilt and fear. The larger narrative from the biblical story is a massive tapestry of grace and generosity. Yahweh bends down and makes clothes for the newly fallen Adam and Eve. God chooses a whining and adulterous band of nomads who frequently go after other gods, and yet Yahweh never gives up on them. The psalmist proclaims the deepest truth about Yahweh: his steadfast love endures forever. The Hebrew word we translate "steadfast love" (*hesed*) occurs 147 times in the Psalms, each time to describe the nature of God. "O give thanks to the God of heaven, / for his steadfast love endures forever" (Psalm 136:26).

They say all musicals can be broken down into "boy meets girl, boy loses girl, boy gets girl." What if you isolated one section, "boy loses girl," and tried to explain the whole story with that single episode? Our understanding would be limited and distorted. The same is true when we take an isolated story that troubles us (for example, Ananias and Sapphira in Acts 5:1-11) and fail to see the entire narrative. If we take an isolated story or verse ("Jacob have I loved, but Esau have I hated" [Romans 9:13 KJV]) and try to build our doctrine of God on it, we commit biblical malpractice. Isolated passages must not rise above their place in the larger narrative. The dominant narrative of the Bible is a story of unearned grace, of a God whose love is not thwarted by human sinfulness, and of a Christ who dies for sinners (Romans 5:8). The minor narratives are a part of the ambiguity of all epic stories.

The metanarrative of the Bible is the story of the steadfast love of God that culminates in the incarnation, death and resurrection of God on behalf of a wayward world. Therefore, we should interpret the entire Bible and each of its parts in light of Jesus. It is noteworthy that every time Paul brings up a story from the Hebrew Bible, he interprets it in light of Jesus. Paul does not retell the story of Abraham by itself. He incorporates the story of Abraham into the story of Jesus. Abraham's faith is like the faith we have in Christ that makes us righteous apart from the law (Romans 4). Adam's fall was not the last word; Adam's sin was overturned by Jesus' sinlessness and self-sacrifice (Romans 5:12-15). Minor narratives must be interpreted in light of the major narrative, and the major narrative of the Bible is grace—undeserved and unearned love.

> If you fell more deeply in love with God, how might that change your behavior?
>
> *[handwritten: We would want to please God more]*

The false narratives we hear in church. Finally, the earning-favor narrative has worked its way into many of our churches. You can hear it proclaimed from many pulpits. Henry Cloud says that if you walk into a given church on Sunday you are apt to hear a message that goes like this: God is good, you are bad, try harder. Because the earning-favor narrative is so familiar, and because guilt and fear and shame are such easy and effective tools of manipulation, preachers have used it to guide people away from the fires of hell and into the bliss of heaven. Citing some of the minor narratives from the Bible, these sermons are crafted to make the hearers a bit uneasy.

I turned on the TV one day and began skimming the channels. I came upon a TV preacher who was reading from Hebrews 6, which was a passage I had been studying that same week, so I was eager to hear how he interpreted it. He read the following passage:

> It is impossible to restore again to repentance those who have once been enlightened, and have tasted the heavenly gift, and have shared in the Holy Spirit, and have tasted the goodness of the word of God and the powers of the age to come, and then have fallen away, since on their own they are crucifying again the Son of God and are holding him up to contempt. (Hebrews 6:4-6)

He took off his glasses and leaned on his pulpit. The camera moved in closer to his face, which was getting red. He looked at the camera and in a voice of quiet trembling asked, "Is this passage describing you?" He paused and glared into the camera, and then blared in a loud and angry voice, "Are you one of those Christians who gave his life to Jesus, who have tasted the goodness of God, and then have *stomped on the blood of Jesus with your sinfulness?*" For the next ten minutes he raged against Christians who sin. Apparently he had stopped sinning some time ago. And even more apparently, Jesus and his Father get really angry if you sin after conversion.

His interpretation of the passage is completely out of context. The major narrative in the epistle to the Hebrews is about the struggle of some of the Jewish Christians who were unable to accept that Jesus' sacrifice was sufficient for all of their sins. Some of them apparently were still going to the temple, making sacrifices of animals and engaging in Jewish rituals to make sure their sins were dealt with and they were in right standing with God. So when the text speaks of those who "have fallen away" (Hebrews 6:6), it is not describing people who were lusting or getting drunk or lying. They were sneaking off to the temple to hedge their bets by offering a goat. They were "crucifying the Son of God" by denying the effectiveness of the cross, as if Jesus had to repeat the crucifixion.

So, how did he get this passage so wrong? Our minds are so accustomed to the earning-favor narrative that we see it even when it is not there. We read words like "fallen away" and make automatic assumptions that this must refer to our sin.

The TV preacher continued to get louder and angrier, until his indictment reached a fever pitch. He pointed his finger at the camera and said, "If you are one of those people who think you are a Christian, but you continue to sin, you are spitting in the face of Jesus, and you will not escape the fires of hell that await you." All of the choir members sitting behind him nervously looked down at their Bibles and jotted notes, deftly avoiding the camera. I was struck by how sad they all seemed. And I was deeply disturbed to have heard a sermon that is completely opposed to the teaching of Jesus.

JESUS' NARRATIVE: THE GENEROUS GOD

I am going to ask you to do something very difficult. I would like for you to let go of everything you think you know about God. I know that sounds impossible, and I suppose it is. But try to imagine that you know nothing about God. You are about to hear Jesus tell a story about God and how he relates to us. Simply listen to Jesus tell you about the God he knows without any preconceived notions.

The kingdom of heaven is like a landowner who went out early in the morning to hire laborers for his vineyard. After agreeing with the laborers for the usual daily wage, he sent them into his vineyard. When he went out about nine o'clock, he saw others standing idle in the marketplace; and he said to them, "You also go into the vineyard, and I will pay you whatever is right." So they went. When he went out again about noon and about three o'clock, he did the same. And about five o'clock he went out and found others standing around; and he said to them, "Why are you standing here idle all day?" They said to him, "Because no one has hired us." He said to them, "You also go into the vine-yard." When evening came, the owner of the vineyard said to his manager, "Call the laborers and give them their pay, beginning with the last and then going to the first." When those hired about five o'clock came, each of them received the usual daily wage. Now when the first came, they thought they would receive more; but each of them also received the usual daily wage. And when they received it, they grumbled against the landowner, saying, "These last worked only one hour, and you have made them equal to us who have borne the burden of the day and the scorching heat." But he replied to one of them, "Friend, I am do-ing you no wrong; did you not agree with me for the usual daily wage? Take what belongs to you and go; I choose to give to this last the same as I give to you. Am I not allowed to do what I choose with what belongs to me? Or are you envious because I am *generous?*" (Matthew 20:1-15, italics added)

A parable of generosity. This is a story Jesus' hearers would have been familiar with. There was a lot of unemployment in Jesus' day, perhaps as many as eighteen thousand men out of work in and around Jerusalem. Each day men would go to the fields looking for work. If they failed to get hired, they went to the marketplace and chatted with one another, hoping to still get a chance to work.

In Jesus' parable a vineyard owner hires a group of men early in the morning, around 6 a.m. These early workers agreed to work for a standard day's wages. Seeing there is much work to be done and not enough time to do it, the owner hires another group, who start around 9 a.m. He does the same at noon, 3 p.m. and finally at 5 p.m. At the end of the day the owner pays the workers. Some have worked twelve or thirteen hours, others have worked for only five or six, and the very last group has only labored for one or two hours. Here comes the shocking part: they all are paid the same amount of money—a standard day's wage! This is stunning and seems highly unfair, so those who worked all day begin to complain. The owner replies, "Friend, I am doing you no wrong; did you not agree with me for the usual daily wage?" The owner concludes with another cutting question: "Are you envious because I am generous?"

Bible scholar Joachim Jeremias notes that a similar parable was told by Jewish rabbis. In their parable the punch line is quite different. The owner of the vineyard explains that the last group got the same amount because they *earned* it—they worked harder and did more in their short time than the first group did all day. Jesus' story is exactly the opposite. It has nothing do with earning, justice or fairness. Jeremias concludes:

> In the parable of Jesus, the labourers who were engaged last show nothing to warrant a claim to a full day's wages; that they receive it is entirely due to the goodness of their employer. Thus in this apparently trivial detail lies the difference between two worlds: the world of merit, and the world of grace; the law contrasted with the gospel. . . . Will you then murmur against God's goodness? That is the core of Jesus' vindication of the gospel: Look what God is like—all goodness.

If this were the only story you knew about God, what would you conclude? I would believe that God does not behave anything like what I see in the world. In our world the parable told by the Jewish rabbis makes sense. The late workers worked harder and got what they deserved. But in Jesus' parable I am struck by the utter gratuity of God. The late workers did not deserve a day's wages! The God Jesus reveals runs counter to the way we are wired to think. Brennan Manning put it succinctly: "Jesus reveals a God who does not demand but who gives; who does not oppress but who raises up; who does not wound but heals; who does not condemn but forgives."

> Do you agree that God is generous and gives to us freely? Why or why not?

We live in a world where people demand, oppress, wound and condemn. In our world we earn what we get. So we project that onto God. It is easy to conceive of a demanding, oppressive, condemning, wounding god who must be appeased. The God Jesus knows is utterly generous.

GENEROSITY AND SCARCITY

Generosity happens when a person is living from a condition of abundance or when a person is moved by the needs of others. If I have three hundred tomatoes, it is easy for me to give dozens away. I have more than I need. I am giving out of my surplus. *Webster's New American Dictionary* defines *generous* as "free in giving or sharing, abundant, ample, bountiful." But I can also be generous even when I have little. I may have only one tomato, but if I see a poor woman who has none, I may very well be moved to give my last tomato to her. Generosity then flows from either a sense of abundance or a feeling of compassion. God is moved by both. God is generous because he lives in a condition of abundance—his provisions can never be exhausted—and God is moved with compassion because he sees our need.

Love and forgiveness, acceptance and kindness, are not commodities that diminish in their giving. When we offer forgiveness we do not have less of it, nor do we diminish our capacity to forgive each time we forgive. So why do we so seldom live generously? We live from a condition of scarcity. We never got enough love from our parents, enough toys on our birthday and enough affirmation from those who know us. Our checking account is limited, and often our money is spent before we earn it. Living from a condition of scarcity, we learn that we must protect what we have. If we give it away, we might end up in dire straits.

I am consistently amazed by how tightfisted and uncharitable we are when it comes to our churches. I had lunch with a pastor who was enraged about the prospect of a new church being built only a few miles from his. He said, "How dare they. Don't they know that this new church will steal some of my people away?" He was operating from a condition of scarcity. He feared their success would make him look like a failure. He was unable to see that the success of this new church was also his success because we are all on the same team. The church is often a place lacking in generosity: *All other churches are wrong. Only we have it right. Our church must succeed. Who cares if theirs fails?*

Our God, however, is constantly generous. Everything we have is a gift. We were made without any effort on our part. We breathe undeserved air. The sun gratuitously rises and warms our planet and, along with the unmerited rain, nourishes the land, yielding delicious fruits and grains. It is all manna, the unearned provision of a lavish and loving God. We have never been and never will be in a place where we can turn to God and say, "You owe me. I deserve this." We do not deserve anything we have been given. We have earned nothing. Yet God continues to give. That is because God is not interested in what we can do for God. God is interested in something much more important than our good works.

What are some ways you have experienced the unearned blessings of God?

WHAT THE GOD OF JESUS REALLY WANTS

Our thinking about life with God inevitably confronts us with this crucial question: *What does God want from me?* When Jesus was asked which was the greatest commandment, he answered clearly: love

God with all you have. If we asked Jesus, What does God want from me? I believe he would answer, *God wants you to know and to love him.* This narrative tells of a God who is loving and merciful, whose desire is to love and to be loved. This in no way negates the fact that God is unflinchingly against sin. God hates sin because it hurts his children. But God is crazy about his children.

The Westminster Larger Catechism, written in 1648, opens with a question and an answer:

Question: What is the chief and highest end of man?

Answer: Man's chief and highest end is to glorify God, and fully to enjoy Him forever.

I love the concept of *fully enjoying God forever.* Do you think that God wants you to enjoy him? Though many people do not believe this, I think it is what God most wants. Julian of Norwich once wrote, "The greatest honor we can give to God is to live gladly because of the knowledge of his love." That statement shocked me when I first read it. The greatest honor we can give to God? Isn't it to die for him on the mission field? Julian offers another narrative: "What God most wants is to see you smile because you know how much God loves you." My mission-field narrative does not describe a God I would naturally love. Julian's narrative tells me of a God I cannot help but love. The God Julian knew is a God who delights in us.

> How does it make you feel to know God delights in you? Why?

THE GOD WHO DELIGHTS IN YOU

A far different narrative about God comes from Kathleen Norris's *Amazing Grace,* where she tells a simple story of discovering God in the face of a child.

One morning this past spring I noticed a young couple with an
infant at an airport departure gate. The baby was staring in-
tently at other people, and as soon as he recognized a human
face, no matter whose it was, no matter if it was young or old,
pretty or ugly, bored or happy or worried-looking he would respond with absolute delight. It was beautiful to see. Our drab
departure gate had become the gate of heaven. And as I watched
that baby play with any adult who would allow it, I felt as awe-
struck as Jacob, because I realized that this is how God looks at
us, staring into our faces in order to be delighted, to see the
creature he made and called good, along with the rest of creation. . . . I suspect that only God, and well-loved infants, can
see this way.

What if God is not mad at you? What if God were actually like the
one in this narrative, a God who responds to us with "absolute delight" regardless of how we look or feel, or what we have or have not
done?

The only possible response would be to feel "absolute delight" in
return. If God is delighted in me—regardless of my performance—
then my immediate response is to feel love in return. And in so doing, I fulfill the greatest commandment. The narrative of the prophet
lady does not lead me to love God, only to fear him. And her narrative uses fear and guilt to get me to change, and does not produce
genuine change. The narrative that God loves us and longs for us to
love him in return provides a genuine and lasting incentive to
change.

Two of the most important verses in the Bible, in my opinion, are
1 John 4:10-11. They are the verses that began my own transformation by the renewing of my mind: "In this is love, not that we loved
God but that he loved us and sent his Son to be the atoning sacrifice
for our sins. Beloved, since God loved us so much, we also ought to
love one another." These verses became the bedrock of my dominant

narrative about God. Our love for God does not determine God's attitude toward us. God loves us first, and we see that clearly in God's Son offering his life in order to reconcile us to God. And that love propels me to love God and others in return. God first loved us and will never stop loving us. The primary thing God wants from us is not improved moral behavior (which will come), but to love God because he first loves us.

THE MOST IMPORTANT THING ABOUT YOU

A. W. Tozer, the great American pastor and devotional writer (1897-1963), wrote:

> What comes into our mind when we think about God is the most important thing about us. . . . Were we able to extract from any man a complete answer to the question, "What comes into your mind when you think about God?" we might predict with certainty the spiritual future of that man.

That is a bold statement: The most important thing about a person is *what they think about God.* After a lot of reflection, I believe he is absolutely right. Our thoughts about God will determine not only who we are but how we live. We *can* predict the "spiritual future" of a person just by knowing what they think about God.

What we think about God—what we think God is like—will determine the relationship we have with God. If we think of God as harsh and demanding, we will probably cower in fear and keep our distance from God. If we think of God as a vague and impersonal force in the universe, we will probably have a vague and impersonal relationship with this god. That's why it's crucial that we have the right thoughts about God. It will determine everything we do. If we have low or false views of God, we are actually

> How do your beliefs about God explain how you live your life?

committing a form of idolatry, worshiping a false god.

What I have discovered is this: when I came to know the God that Jesus revealed, I absolutely fell in love with God. The more I grasp about the nature and work of the triune God, the more I am enthralled with the truth, goodness and beauty of the Father, Son and Holy Spirit. I want to turn your attention to the God Jesus reveals. His God is good and beautiful, loving and trustworthy, self-sacrificial and forgiving, powerful and caring, and out for our good. I hope that when you finish this book, you will have fallen in love with the God Jesus knows, and that you will wake up inspired and enthused about living another day with this good and beautiful and generous God.

praying psalm 23

Psalm 23 is a beautiful expression of the kingdom of God, in which God is with us, caring and providing for us, and blessing us, even in trying circumstances. The God of Psalm 23 is generous. Because of God's gracious provision, protection and care, we lack nothing. God invites us to rest, to be refreshed and to be restored. God leads and guides us, even in our most painful situations. And because God is with us, we can live without fear. God even prepares a "table" for us in the presence of those who would harm us. God not only provides what we need, he gives us more than we need—our cup is overflowing. When we walk with God as our Shepherd, we see our entire life—even our trials and suffering—as goodness and mercy.

This psalm is read at nearly every Christian funeral because it provides comfort, especially the verse about walking in the valley of death and not being afraid. But this psalm is not primarily for funerals but for everyday life. As you go about your week, carry this psalm with you and recite it as often as you can.

> The LORD is my shepherd, I shall not want.
>   He makes me lie down in green pastures;
>   he leads me beside still waters;
>   he restores my soul.
>   He leads me in right paths
>   for his name's sake.

Even though I walk through the darkest valley,
> I fear no evil;
for you are with me;
> your rod and your staff—
> they comfort me.

You prepare a table before me
> in the presence of my enemies;
you anoint my head with oil;
> my cup overflows.
Surely goodness and mercy shall follow me
> all the days of my life,
and I shall dwell in the house of the LORD
> my whole life long. (Psalm 23)

Try to recite this psalm before you fall asleep each night, and again when you awake. Before your feet hit the ground, try to have slowly meditated on each word. Recite it so often this week that it becomes second nature to you, as natural as breathing. You will notice yourself beginning to pray it at odd times.

HOW DOES THIS EXERCISE HELP TRAIN MY SOUL?

This psalm contains a narrative about the exceedingly generous God. By letting the images wash over your mind, you imbed this true narrative into your soul. Your mind and your body will begin to be shaped by these words. As you begin you will probably have to refocus your attention, but it soon turns into a prayer experience.

FOR REFLECTION

Whether you are going through this material alone or with others, the following questions might be helpful as you reflect on your experience. Either way, it might be a good idea to answer these questions in your journal. If you are meeting with a group, bring your journal with you to help you remember your insights as you share your experiences.

1. Were you able to practice the exercise this week? If so, describe
   what you did and how you felt about it.

2. What, if anything, did you learn about God or yourself through
   the exercise?

3. What was the most meaningful verse or phrase of Psalm 23 for
   you?

five

god is love

My friend and pastor Jeff Gannon was sitting in his office one afternoon when the phone rang. The young woman on the phone said, "I just have a question. May I come to your church?"

Jeff was stunned by the question. "Can you come to our church? Of course you can. Why would you even feel a need to ask such a question?" he asked.

"Let me tell you my story before you answer," she said.

The young woman went on to tell him that when she was a junior in high school she got pregnant by a young man who had no interest in her or the baby she was carrying. She decided not to get an abortion and, after some soul searching, began to feel a need to get her life in order. She went back to the church she had gone to when she was a young girl, and started to feel that she was on the right track.

After a few months of attending church she thought that other girls might benefit from her mistakes, so she asked the pastor if she could speak to the middle-school girls about the pressures of dating and sex. The pastor said to her, "No, I would never allow that. I am afraid that your type of person might rub off on them." Though she felt rejected, she also felt at home in that church, so she kept attending. A few months after her baby was born, she called the pastor to schedule a Sunday on which she could have her baby baptized. The pastor said, "That is not going to happen in my church. I would never baptize an illegitimate baby."

"Now that you know my story," she said to Jeff, "can I still come to your church?"

FALSE NARRATIVE

To some people the reaction of the pastor who rejected the young woman seems shocking and insensitive (which it is), but in truth, it reflects a dominant narrative among many Christians (and non-Christians): God only loves us when we're good.

Many people live with the assumption that God's love is conditional. Our behavior, it's assumed, determines how God feels about us. Consequently, God's love is constantly in flux. It's as if God were on a kind of swivel chair, looking at us and smiling when we keep our minds, hands and hearts pure, but the moment we sin God turns his back on us. The only way to get God to turn back to us is by resuming our good behavior. I know this narrative firsthand. The god I created in my mind years ago was spinning so much it made me dizzy to watch.

Have you heard something similar to the swivel-chair narrative in your own life? Please describe it.

THE WORLD OF PERFORMANCE-BASED ACCEPTANCE

Not long after we're born we discover that the world we live in is based on *performance*. Our parents begin molding and shaping our behavior from a very early age. Some of the first words we learn are *good* and *bad*. We hear things like "Oh, you ate all of your peas—*good* girl" or "Do not write on the wall with your crayon—*bad* boy." Before we can speak, we become aware that acceptance hinges on our behavior, which produces a decidedly unstable world of highly conditional love.

As a parent it's easy to promote this narrative. I watch over my children, and when they do something well I'm quick to affirm it. Conversely, when they do something wrong they're certain to hear about it. No matter how much I try to avoid it, it comes out. Part of this is necessary because a parent's job is to teach right and wrong; the difficulty is making it clear to my children that their actions and not their identity is being evaluated.

While this narrative of performance-based acceptance begins in our families, it is no different outside our homes. The world we live in reinforces performance-based acceptance. If we do well in school we're praised; if we score the winning basket we're admired; and if we are handsome or beautiful we're affirmed. Our acceptance, our value and our worth, we quickly discern, are based on external talents and abilities and performance.

Because this is so much a part of the way we see and experience the world, it is only natural that we project this same understanding onto God. God is bigger, smarter and more powerful than our parents, the coach and the boss. God sees everything! What can we do to get God to approve of, accept and love us? The answer, as you would expect, has to do with our *religious performance*. If you ask the average person, "What must you do to get God to like, favor and bless you?" the answer would be clear and consistent: "Well, I

> Has the performance-based narrative been part of your experience? Can you think of an example of this in your own life?

think I would have to go to church, read my Bible, give some money, serve on committees and serve the needy. Oh, and God does not want me to sin—or at least keep it at a minimum."

Thus we can control how God feels about us by doing those things on the list and avoiding sin. This is *legalism*, the attempt to earn God's love through our actions, to earn God's favor or avoid God's curses through pious activities. In the end, legalism is superstition, not unlike avoiding black cats and ladders. We are drawn to superstitious and legalistic behaviors because they provide a sense of control in an otherwise chaotic world. But God's favor is not earned by what we do any more than good luck is found in a rabbit's foot.

> Do you sometimes feel that God's love depends on your behavior?

Performance-based acceptance (legalism) is a dominant narrative for many of us despite the fact that it leaves us in a state of constant uncertainty and anxiety. The good news is that this is not Jesus' narrative. In fact, he seemed to go out of his way, in both words and actions, to tell the opposite story about God.

JESUS' NARRATIVES

In my search of Scripture I was unable to find a passage in which Jesus tells us that God only likes us when we're good or when we engage in pious activities. Instead he tells of a God who offers unconditional acceptance to all people. But before we look at his words, let's look at his *actions*.

A God who welcomes sinners. Jesus not only reveals the Father in his stories, he reflects the Father in his character and his actions. The following story from Matthew's Gospel tells us a lot about the Father whom Jesus reveals.

> As Jesus was walking along, he saw a man called Matthew sitting at the tax booth; and he said to him, "Follow me." And he got up and followed him.
> And as he sat at dinner in the house, many tax collectors and sinners came and were sitting with him and his disciples. When

the Pharisees saw this, they said to his disciples, "Why does your teacher eat with tax collectors and sinners?" But when he heard this, he said, "Those who are well have no need of a physician, but those who are sick. Go and learn what this means, 'I desire mercy, not sacrifice.' For I have come to call not the righteous but sinners." (Matthew 9:9-13)

Matthew was a tax collector, which was a despicable occupation for Jewish men. Tax collectors typically sat in roadside booths, like tollbooths, collecting taxes from the Jewish people for the Roman government. They worked for the "bad guys," so to speak. But even worse, they were notorious for skimming money off the top for themselves. They were thought of as traitors *and* cheats—not a great combination.

In this passage Jesus invites Matthew, a tax collector, to be one of his disciples. This is amazing, considering that in the first century, a rabbi was usually very selective when choosing his disciples. Being selected by a rabbi was a rare and great privilege that was offered only to those who were deemed especially righteous. Jesus' choice is therefore ludicrous and shocking.

After being chosen, Matthew invites Jesus to dine with him in his home. This is a sign of his allegiance to Jesus, his new rabbi. Naturally, Matthew's friends are tax collectors and other kinds of "sinners." Jesus dines with these sinners, which is a sign of love and acceptance. The Pharisees, a group of strict religious men, had been keeping an eye on Jesus for some time, and when they catch him eating with sinners they're sure they have exposed him as a false prophet, a fake, a charlatan, a hypocrite.

> If someone were to look at the kind of people you spend time with, what would they assume about your main narratives?

But Jesus says to them that he has not come for the healthy but for the sick, not for the righteous but for the unrighteous. The irony of the story is that the Pharisees are just as sick and sinful as the tax collectors; they just fail to admit it. The tax collectors, on the other hand, have no pretense. They're used to being called sinners. Their only question is why they're invited to the party.

If Jesus reached out to known scoundrels, then the rest of us have a chance. As Brennan Manning writes of the passage we've been looking at:

> Here is the revelation bright as the evening star: Jesus comes for sinners, for those as outcast as tax collectors and for those caught up in squalid choices and failed dreams. He comes for corporate executives, street people, superstars, farmers, hookers, addicts, IRS agents, AIDS victims, and even used car salesmen. . . . This passage should be read, reread, and memorized. Every Christian generation tried to dim the blinding brightness of its meaning because the gospel seems too good to be true.

Why do we, as Manning notes, try to "dim" this message? Why does it seem "too good to be true"? Because Jesus' narrative of unconditional acceptance goes against the grain of the performance-based-acceptance narrative that is so deeply embedded in our lives. How could God possibly *love* sinners? He might be able to forgive them and even love them *if they promise to improve*. But this is not what Jesus taught. In actions and words he proclaimed that God loves sinners—as they are, and not as they should be.

God loves sinners. In what is probably the most famous of all of the verses in the Bible, Jesus tells us:

> For God so loved the world that he gave his only Son, so that everyone who believes in him may not perish but may have eternal life.
>
> Indeed, God did not send the Son into the world to condemn the world, but in order that the world might be saved through him. (John 3:16-17)

This passage has brought comfort to countless people, and is considered by many to be a summation of the entire Bible. Jesus is explaining the reason for his mission: God loved the world and wanted to save it. Many people believe that God is mad at them, but for some reason he has yet to punish them fully. Such people would be more comfortable had Jesus said, "For God was so mad at the world that he sent his Son to come down and tell them to shape up, that whosoever would shape up would have eternal life. Indeed, God did send his Son into the world to condemn it, in order that the world might be saved through good works."

Jesus does not say that God loved "a few," or "some" or even "many." He says God loved the *world*. And the world, as we know it, is full of sinners. Therefore, God must love sinners. Jesus did not say, "For God so loved the good people, the righteous people, the religious people, that he gave his only Son." He said God loved the world—an all-inclusive world of sinners. The apostle Paul echoes this when he writes, "But God proves his love for us in that while we still were sinners Christ died for us" (Romans 5:8).

God loves in spite of the broken and sinful condition of the beloved, and this is the only real proof of genuine love. The most well-known of all Jesus' parables is a story about a father and his two sons, which resonates with our deep yearning to be loved by God without condition.

THE PRODIGAL FATHER

The parable of the prodigal son should really be called the parable of the father's love. The word *prodigal* means "recklessly extravagant." We attach the word to the younger son, the one in the story who spends all of his inheritance on sinful living. But it is the father who is the most recklessly extravagant, offering his wealth to an ungrateful son and lavishly loving the son when he returns. The story is familiar to most Christians, but I want to point out a few important aspects of the story that heighten Jesus' teaching about his Father (see Luke 15:11-32).

We have heard this parable so many times that the shocking parts of it are often unnoticed. The younger of two sons asks his father for his inheritance so he can go off on his own. This was a stunning and disrespectful request, and yet the father grants it to him. The younger son then wastes all of his money on sinful living and eventually hits rock bottom. The only job he can find is feeding pigs, and while dining on their slop he becomes sick. In a moment of reflection the younger son decides that his father's servants are better off than he is, so he composes a confession he will make to his father, asking to be one of his servants.

Then the story takes another surprising turn. In what I think is one of the most beautiful verses in the Bible, we read, "But while he was still far off, his father saw him and was filled with compassion" (Luke 15:20). We are given the sense that this father has been looking for his son's return, perhaps every day. And when he sees the son he is "filled with compassion." This is no small detail; it tells us about the character and heart of God. God looks at us with compassion, even when we have done the very worst to God we could possibly do.

In the world of Jesus' day the father had a right to take his son before the elders and have him stoned, perhaps even to death. No one would have questioned the father had he done this. Justice would have been served (a natural narrative). But instead, the father hugs the son—and kisses him, which is a sign of forgiveness—welcomes him home and throws him a party. He asks for his servants to bring his son a robe, a ring and a pair of shoes—three signs of restored sonship. He has all the rights of a son; his position has been restored; he has lost nothing. And he deserves none of it.

> Have you ever been in a position to love someone who rejected you? Or have you ever been loved by someone you have hurt? Describe.

God, it appears, is very fond of sinners. Not their sin. The father obviously was grieved over his son's decisions; he neither endorsed nor overlooked the son's reckless living. Any good father would be rightly upset by the actions of the younger son. But Jesus wants us to understand that even the worst of our sins will not prevent God from loving us or stop God from longing for our return. The parable is not so much about a sinner getting saved as it is about a God who loves even those who sin against him.

THE ELDER BROTHER AND ME

Remember, Jesus tells this parable in response to the criticism that he's dining with sinners. Luke sets the scene for us: "Now all the tax collectors and sinners were coming near to listen to him. And the Pharisees and the scribes were grumbling and saying, 'This fellow welcomes sinners and eats with them' " (Luke 15:1-2). As noted earlier, Jesus' actions were revolutionary. No rabbi would dine with known sinners, and the Pharisees openly criticized him for it.

Most of us tend to focus on the prodigal son and the father, but the second half of the parable (Luke 15:25-32) reveals Jesus' primary storytelling aim. This parable was not directed to the downtrodden and marginalized as much as it was to the upright and the pious who could not accept the radical message of God's unconditional love. The character of the elder brother represents those of us who chafe at the idea of God loving sinners. The elder brother represents the part of us that is not comfortable with God's unconditional love for others or even ourselves.

The elder son is working in the field when he hears a party going on. He comes in the house to discover a feast in his younger brother's honor. So he complains to his father, "This is unfair! I work hard every day and I've never been given a party like this! This horrible son of yours—I refuse to call him 'brother'—nearly ruined our estate and spent it on whores, and you give him a feast?" The elder brother has a right to be angry. He has never disrespected his father. He has never hurt the family financially. He has never acted selfishly. And yet the younger son, who has done all of that and more, gets a hero's welcome.

The father reminds the elder son that there is no injustice in his actions. He says, "All that is mine is yours." In other words, you have the same things your brother has. This is similar to the parable of the workers in the vineyard who worked different amounts for the same wage. Jesus is striking at the heart of the problem we have with grace: we don't like it. It seems unfair, but in reality it is perfectly fair. God is gracious to all. It smacks against our performance-based-acceptance narrative.

> Do you sometimes feel like the elder brother in the story who is reluctant to accept God's acceptance of others or even yourself?

The chief point is that there is only one thing that separates us from God, and it is not our sin. It is our self-righteousness. Our self-righteousness does not turn God from us, but us from God. It is not my sin that moves me away from God, it is my refusal of grace, both for myself and for others. The father tells the older son that the return of his younger son is cause for celebration and rejoicing. Jesus is speaking to the Pharisees, essentially saying, "When you see the tax collectors, the prostitutes and the other known sinners coming to me, you should rejoice—they were dead and now are alive. Instead, you grumble."

The Pharisees had to decide whether to accept that God welcomes sinners and to share in their joy. Sadly, they refused. I am more like the elder brother (the Pharisees) than the prodigal son. But God's grace toward sinners is not what troubles me; it is God's grace toward *me* that I sometimes have difficulty with. My earning-favor narrative is so deeply embedded in my theological template that I find God's love difficult. That is why I was so moved by a poem I discovered in a dusty old library book.

THE TRUTH ABOUT GOD

Several years ago I was reading about Simone Weil, a writer whose work I had recently come to appreciate. Her books reveal her deep thinking and devout faith. She was raised in a Jewish family, but became a Christian later in life. Her biographer noted that she became a Christian when she read a poem by a seventeenth-century pastor named George Herbert. The poem is Herbert's third poem on love.

I quickly went to the library and checked out a book of Herbert's poems. I sat down to read the poem, and I too was so moved that I could hardly speak for a few moments. The more I read and thought about it, the more I realized just how profound it is.

Love (III)
Love bade me welcome, yet my soul drew back,
 Guilty of dust and sin.
But quick-ey'd Love, observing me grow slack
 From my first entrance in,
Drew nearer to me, sweetly questioning
 If I lack'd any thing.

"A guest," I answer'd, "worthy to be here";
 Love said, "You shall be he."
"I, the unkind, ungrateful? ah my dear,
 I cannot look on thee."
Love took my hand, and smiling did reply,
 "Who made the eyes but I?"

"Truth, Lord, but I have marr'd them; let my shame
 Go where it doth deserve."
"And know you not," says Love, "who bore the blame?"
 "My dear, then I will serve."
"You must sit down," says Love, "and taste my meat."
 So I did sit and eat.

FINIS
Glory to God on high, and on earth peace,
Good will towards men.

Since the poem is quite old and the language is difficult, I would
like to explain what the poem means (at least to me) in an attempt to
offer some insights into it.

- *Love bade me welcome.* Right away Herbert tells us about the nature
  of God. The poet agrees with John—God *is* love (1 John 4:8).
  Throughout the poem you could substitute the word *love* with the
  word *God.* The poet is saying, "God bade me welcome." God invites us in.

- *Yet my soul drew back.* But what is the soul's response? When God
  draws near—really near—it is natural and even right for us to
  draw back. God is, after all, holy and righteous.

- *Guilty of dust and sin.* Herbert tells us why we draw back; he never
  says we are anything other than guilty. You and I all know in our
  heart of hearts that we have failed, that we have fallen short of
  God countless times, and we draw back because we are guilty.

- *But quick-ey'd Love.* Herbert describes God's sight as "quick-eyed
  Love." Isn't that beautiful? God sees us fully and completely. He
  watches us, yes, but with eyes of love and compassion.

- *Observing me grow slack / From my first entrance in.* Growing slack,
  in Herbert's day, meant hesitation. Do you see the movement? God
  invites us in, but we draw back. God knows why—we feel guilty.
  So what does God do?

- *Drew nearer to me.* God comes closer. He sees us falter and steps toward us. Even as we faint and fall away, God draws closer to us.

- *Sweetly questioning.* God sweetly questions us. Here begins a kind
  of gentle argument. God draws near and asks us a question. With
  my earning-favor narrative well in place, I am sure God will ask,
  "Why have you sinned so much?" But it is not so.

- *If I lack'd any thing.* God's first question is not, "What do you have to say for yourself, you rotten sinner?" but rather, "What do you lack? Do you need something?"

- *"A guest," I answer'd, "worthy to be here."* We lack a sense of being worthy. Most of us feel unworthy before God. The speaker is telling the truth.

- *Love said, "You shall be he."* Love responds to our doubts about our worthiness by saying, "You are worthy. You are because I say you are. You are because of my love for you." Augustine once wrote, "By loving us, God makes us lovable." Our worthiness will never be merited, achieved or earned. It is given to us as a gift, and a gift can only be received.

- *"I, the unkind, ungrateful? ah my dear, / I cannot look on thee."* But we have a hard time receiving gifts. After all, the whole world runs on merit, on earning what we get. So we respond, "Who . . . me? I, the ungrateful, the unkind? Do you really know how bad I am, God? I cannot even look at you!"

- *Love took my hand, and smiling did reply, / "Who made the eyes but I?"* This is a shocking image. Can you imagine God smiling—about anything? About you? Many people I know cannot imagine that God is proud of them, that God even likes them. And look at God's marvelous response: "Who made your eyes—wasn't it me?" We say, "God, I am unworthy to look at you," and God replies, "Can't you understand that those eyes, the ones you can't lift up to me—*I made them!*"

- *"Truth, Lord, but I have marr'd them."* "Yes," we answer. We cannot argue with God on this one. "But [there is always a 'but'] I have marr'd them." Hebert is saying, "Yes, you made my eyes, God, but I have not used them rightly. I have looked on things I should not have; I have marred them by my own actions."

- *"Let my shame / Go where it doth deserve."* Once again, the poor soul argues, "God, do you know who you are talking to? I am a mess. You gave me my eyes—my everything—and I have ruined them. So, please, let my shame go where it deserves." It is here in the poem that the soul cries out not for mercy but for justice: "I am not worthy—give me not what I want but what I deserve."

- *"And know you not,"* says Love, *"who bore the blame?"* When we reach this important place, God steps in and says, "I will not disagree. You have failed. And you deserve to be punished for it. But—pay attention to this—do you not know who bore the blame?" God is saying, "Jesus bore the blame. My Son took your shame, and you bear it no more."

We need to stop here for a moment. Sometimes people talk about God's love as being this cosmic good feeling toward all people with no regard for justice, as though sin were no big deal. This is why many do not think of themselves as sinners. But notice: if you are not a sinner, then why do you feel so bad? And if you pretend you are a sinner, then you will have to pretend you are forgiven. God says, "Your sin is real. The penalty is death. But my Son, Jesus, took the blame. He nailed your sins to his cross. He is 'the judge judged in our place.' "

- *"My dear, then I will serve."* Quite often the message of grace makes us feel guilty, instead of making us feel joyful and free. And there are many preachers who preach with that effect in mind: "Don't you know, young man, that Jesus died for you—don't you feel guilty about that?" And the intended response is, "Yes, yes I do. I'm sorry, Lord. I promise to do better. I'll try harder to do better— I promise! I'll even die on a mission field for you. Just give me a command, and I'll do it. I owe you, God."

- *"You must sit down,"* says Love, *"and taste my meat."* In response God says, "Sit down. Rest here. Feast with me. *Be* with me. Enjoy my presence, and let *me* serve *you* first. I don't need you to serve me. I don't need you for anything. I made you because I love you, and what I really want is to be with you. My deepest desire is not that you go off to try to serve me, but that you would let me love you."

What do you think God wants most from you?

- *So I did sit and eat.* This is what God wants most of all. He wants to serve us, to see us feast and rejoice in his goodness. One day we will serve others, but only as a response to God's love, not motivated by guilt.

George Herbert was a brilliant politician who left it all to be the pastor of a small church. He wrote many poems, but never intended for them to be read, much less published. On his deathbed he told a close friend that he had a number of poems he had written, and said, "Please read them, and if you think they might be useful, do with them what you will."

His poems were published posthumously. I was stunned by his modest words: "If you think they might be useful." I thank God that his friend had the wisdom to see that they would indeed be useful. I know Simone Weil felt the same way I do.

LEGALISM LIMITS; LOVE COMPELS

This chapter opened with the story of a young woman who became pregnant out of wedlock and was shunned by her pastor when she wanted to help the young women in the youth group. The pastor also refused to baptize her baby. She ended up in another church, and her child was baptized not long after. She worked with young people, finished her education and eventually went into mission work. Today she and her daughter live and work as missionaries in Africa.

SOUL TRAINING

Lectio Divina

The spiritual exercise for this week is called *lectio divina*, which is a Latin term literally meaning "divine reading." It is a method of reading the Bible that involves listening with the heart. It's an ancient practice that goes all the way back to the Hebraic tradition of the *Shema*, which involved reading select passages of the Hebrew Bible with specific pauses and concentration on certain words. *Lectio divina* was practiced in a communal way by Christians in the early church and was later taught by the desert fathers and mothers with an emphasis on the individual.

In *lectio divina* we turn to a passage of the Bible—usually no more than a few verses—and read it over and over, very slowly, reflecting on each word and phrase, all the while paying attention to the impact the words have on our hearts. In this way we are "praying the Scriptures." It is very different from studying Scripture, in which we come to the text to try to understand its meaning. In *lectio divina*, the Bible passage "studies us."

HOW TO PRACTICE *LECTIO DIVINA*

1. First, select a passage of the Bible. In this specific exercise, I have chosen 1 Corinthians 13:4-8.

Love is patient, love is kind. It does not envy, it does not boast, it is not proud. It is not rude, it is not self-seeking, it is not easily angered, it keeps no record of wrongs. Love does not delight in evil but rejoices with the truth. It always protects, always trusts, always hopes, always perseveres. Love never fails. (1 Corinthians 13:4-8 NIV) *or find another that speaks to you.*

2. Spend a minute or two just relaxing and breathing deeply.

3. *First reading.* Read the passage through, one time, slowly. Pause between each clause (for example, "Love is patient," [pause] "Love is kind," [pause] . . .). After you finish this first reading, be silent for a minute or two.

4. *Second reading.* Read the text slowly once again, pausing between phrases. But this time pause even longer and be aware if any of the words or phrases catch your attention, or seem to stand out in some way. Make a mental note of those. After you finish the second reading, write down those special words or phrases.

5. *Third reading.* Reread the passage up to the word or phrase that touched you in some way. When you reach that word or phrase, stop and repeat it a few times.

6. *Pondering.* Reflect for a while on the phrase that moved you. Repeat it a few more times. Let the words interact with your thoughts, your memories or any other Bible passages that come to mind. Let it touch your heart, desires and fears. Begin to wonder, *What might God want to say to me specifically?*

7. *Prayer.* Turn that last question into a prayer, asking God, "What is the word you have for me in this passage, God? Is there anything you want to say to me today?" Listen. Write down anything you sense God might be saying to you.

8. *Rest.* Be still and silent for a while. Enjoy being in the presence of God. In this step you move from doing to being. Simply be for a while.

9. *Response.* Ask yourself and God, *What am I being called to do as a result of the word I have been given?* Perhaps you are feeling challenged to love God more, or to accept some aspect of who you are, or to serve someone you know, or to begin changing some aspect of your character. Whatever it is, write it out. "Today God is calling me to be a more patient person. Be with me God, and teach me how." Thank God for the word and the calling you have been given.

*Read the following section only after you have completed the exercise.

CONNECTING WITH JESUS' NARRATIVE

Lectio divina is a very personal activity, so I cannot predict exactly what you will experience, nor should I. I imagine God had a specific word just for you. However, the passage I have chosen for you deals specifically with love. First Corinthians 13:4-8 is well known because it is read at many weddings. The context of the passage is not about the love between a husband and a wife (though that fits!), but rather Paul is writing about how to live together in Christian community. The central point is that love is at the core of our life together. Elsewhere we read that we ought to love one another as God has loved us (1 John 4:11).

We also read that "God is love" (1 John 4:8). As with the Herbert poem, it is possible to insert *God* for the word *love* in the passage from 1 Corinthians.

God is patient, God is kind. God does not envy, God does not boast, God is not proud. God is not rude, God is not self-seeking, God is not easily angered, God keeps no record of wrongs. God does not delight in evil but rejoices with the truth. God always protects, always trusts, always hopes, always perseveres. God never fails.

You might enjoy reading over this passage a few times this week. I have said in this chapter that God is love, but often we don't know what that means. This passage explains what true love is.

ADDITIONAL EXERCISE: REFLECTING ON THE POEM

If the subject of God's unconditional love is something you have wrestled with, you may also want to go back to the Herbert poem and reflect some more on it. Read it over slowly and reflect on some of the images Herbert offers (for example, "quick-ey'd love") and try to picture them with your mind's eye.

FOR REFLECTION

Whether you are going through this material alone or with others, the following questions might be helpful as you reflect on your experience. Either way, it might be a good idea to answer these questions in your journal. If you are meeting with a group, bring your journal with you to help you remember your insights as you share your experiences.

1. Were you able to do the *lectio divina* exercise? If so, describe how it went and how you felt about it.

2. What, if anything, did you learn about God or yourself through the exercise?

3. What was your favorite line in the poem "Love (III)"? Explain why.

god is Holy

I was preaching at a church five years after having preached there once before. Because I have a limited repertoire, I was giving a similar message to the one I had given previously. I was hoping that in the years that had passed the congregation would have experienced a slight case of amnesia. I related to the church some of the concepts you have already read in this book: God loves you without condition; Jesus died for all of your sins—God has reconciled you to himself; and in Christ you are a new creation. After the service, a large and powerful man came up to me, looked at me and held out an electronic device to me without saying a word. I looked closely at it, and on it was the sermon I had given five years earlier. I immediately assumed he was going to mock me for preaching essentially the same sermon.

"I apologize for preaching such a similar sermon—but you have to understand, I only have one sermon, I suppose."

I looked at his face and noticed a tear falling down his cheek.

"I didn't come up to tease you about your sermon being the same, but to thank you. I heard this message five years ago, and it changed my life completely. I grew up in a highly legalistic church, and every week I heard about how God was mad at me, and how I was not good enough. I lived every day in fear of God, and I didn't love God at all. When I heard your sermon it melted my heart. I bought the CD and downloaded it, and have listened to it dozens of times, and have given it away to just about everyone I know. I'm a police officer, so I'm not used to being so emotional. I just wanted to thank you for this message."

We gave each other a big bear hug, and he wept. I was overcome by his story and overwhelmed by his emotions. After he walked away, I basked in the glow of knowing that I had actually made a difference in someone's life, and I turned to God and silently thanked him.

This reinforced in my mind just how life-changing this message is about a God who loves us without condition.

Then I noticed a young woman who was waiting to speak with me, so I stepped to where she was standing and introduced myself. She then said, with a huge smile on her face, "Thank you so much for that sermon. It was very freeing!"

The glow returned for a moment, until she went on.

"You see," she said, "I've been living with my boyfriend for the past six months, and I was raised in a church that said this was a sin, and I felt really guilty. But this morning you said that God loves us without condition, and that Jesus has forgiven all of our sins, and then I realized that my guilt was unnecessary. Jesus paid it all! So I just wanted to say thank you for such a liberating message." She shook my hand and started to walk away with a bounce in her step, like a woman who has just been told by her doctor that she is cancer-free.

My heart sank.

I realized then that simply proclaiming the good news that God loves us no matter what we do is not the whole story. What she failed to understand, and what I later was able to explain to her, is that our loving God is also "a consuming fire" (Hebrews 12:29). That may sound daunting, but it is actually very good news. There was much I needed to explain to that young woman about the holiness and purity of God. Fortunately, that brief interaction was not our last discussion.

FALSE NARRATIVES

So far I have been trying to expose some of the dark and negative narratives about God we hear in religious circles—the angry god who judges us harshly, the god who must be prodded and cajoled into forgiving even our minor infractions. I have tried to show that this is not the God Jesus knows and loves and proclaims. Instead, God's love is not contingent on anything we do. God *is* love. God even loves sinners. However, the fact that God loves sinners is usually followed with, "But God still hates sin." That narrative, I believe, is absolutely true.

It has been my experience that people hold one of two dominant narratives, and both of them are wrong.

God is wrathful. There are those who think God is mad all the time, that wrath and anger are essential to God's nature because God is holy and so much of the world is not. One woman said to me, "I just figure that God is generally angry with me, but puts up with it until I do something really bad, and then I wonder, 'Oh no, what is God going to do to me?' " Her narrative is very common. God, people assume, is mad at all of the sin he sees and is ready to bring the divine hammer down when he gets really fed up. However, the Bible also says, "God so loved the world" and "in Christ God was reconciling the world." This is where the narrative gets modified: God the Father is really angry at our sin and would send us to hell, except his Son, Jesus, stepped in and took the punishment for us. This is how people balance God's anger and forgiveness.

> Has the wrath of God been hard for you to understand? Explain.

God does not care about our sin. But there is another narrative that is also popular, especially in our postmodern world. Today many people have abandoned the "angry God" narratives, believing that God is just the opposite. In our day you are just as likely to hear a person tell you that their god is a cosmic, benevolent spirit who never judges, does not punish sin and sends no one to hell. This "teddy bear" god has become a very fashionable alternative to the wrathful god of days gone by.

If you watch popular TV talk shows, you will often hear this god mentioned. The appeal is easy to understand. A loving spirit who wants to bless everyone is certainly preferable to the "Marquis de God," who is cruel and sadistic, ready to send a person into eternal torment for having the wrong doctrine or for failing to overcome some sin. But is this benign spirit the biblical God? Is that narrative any closer to Jesus' narrative concerning his Father? The cushy, fuzzy god is neither biblical nor truly loving.

H. Richard Niebuhr, the great professor of theology and ethics who taught at Yale University for decades, nailed this problem with his famous and insightful observation that the modern religious narrative teaches that "a God without wrath brought men without sin into a kingdom without judgment through the ministrations of a Christ without a Cross."

> What examples of the teddy-bear understanding of God have you experienced?

This quote shows how several narratives in orthodox Christianity hang together, of necessity, around the issue of sin. The narrative of a god who does not care about sin naturally undermines the entire Christian story. God demonstrates wrath toward sin; there is judgment in God's kingdom, and there is a need for Jesus to die on a cross.

The teddy-bear god seems inviting at first. But when you look at our world or look deeply into your own heart, you see a darkness that is unmistakable. The nonwrathful god is powerless against this darkness. As strange as it may sound, in my understanding, the wrath of God is a beautiful part of the majesty and love of God. Before I explain why, we need to turn once again to Jesus to get a balanced view of the character of God.

JESUS' NARRATIVE: WRATH IS GOD'S RIGHT ACTION

We often think of Jesus as meek and mild, as one who strolled through the lilies of the field and talked of peace and love. Or of a Jesus who whistled while he worked as the birds perched upon his shoulders and the mice helped him in the carpenter's shop. (No wait, that's Cinderella I'm thinking of.) Nonetheless, we are more comfortable with a Mr. Rogers kind of Jesus than the one who actually appears in the pages of the Bible. In order to balance that perspective we need to look at what Jesus had to say about judgment and wrath. The following five passages reveal another dimension to God.

> Do not be astonished at this; for the hour is coming when all who are in their graves will hear his voice and will come out— those who have done good, to the resurrection of life, and those who have done evil, to the resurrection of *condemnation*. (John 5:28, italics added)

> I tell you, on the day of judgment you will have to give an account for every careless word you utter; for by your words you will be justified, and by your words you will be *condemned*. (Matthew 12:36-37, italics added)

> For the Son of Man is to come with his angels in the glory of his Father, and then he will *repay* everyone for what has been done. (Matthew 16:27, italics added)

> Woe to those who are pregnant and to those who are nursing infants in those days! For there will be great distress on the earth and *wrath* against this people. (Luke 21:23, italics added)

> Whoever believes in the Son has eternal life; whoever disobeys
> the Son will not see life, but must endure God's *wrath*. (John
> 3:36, italics added)

Words like *condemnation* and *wrath* are not often associated with
Jesus. But we cannot overlook the fact that he spoke often about these
things. How do we integrate these teachings with those we have
looked at so far? How do we
make sense of a God who, according to Jesus, is like a father
who would throw a party for a
wayward son, and yet at the
same time feels wrath toward
those who reject him? To do so we need to take a closer look at what
Jesus means by *condemnation* and *wrath*.

> Why do we skip over Jesus'
> words of judgment to dwell
> on his words about love?

Integrating God's love and his wrath is difficult. Most people don't;
they simply decide to go one way or the other. But it is something we
must do because Jesus does not allow us to choose one or the other.
He speaks of God as being both, and both is what we need to have a
full understanding of God. As Paul said, "Note then the *kindness* and
the *severity* of God: severity toward those who have fallen, but God's
kindness toward you" (Romans 11:22, italics added).

God is both kind and severe. We cannot have one without the
other. In actuality, this is *very* good news.

PASSION VERSUS PATHOS

The great American statesman and president Thomas Jefferson was a
man of science who did not believe in miracles but really liked Jesus.
Unfortunately, right next to Jesus' ethical teachings are stories about
miracles—feeding five thousand people with a sack lunch, walking
on water, curing blindness. Jefferson resolved this conflict in a very
pragmatic way. He took a pair of scissors and cut out the miracle
stories. He was left with the teachings of Jesus. He also snipped out

some of those teachings that were a bit incredible. In the end he had just the Jesus he wanted.

It's easy to do this. I suppose I do it in my own way, though not with scissors. I just skip over the parts I don't like and camp out in the passages I do. This has not been a good strategy, however. I have found that in so doing I lose some important aspect of God or of the Christian life. And that missing piece can make all the difference.

A person similar to Jefferson is the nineteenth-century theologian Albrecht Ritschl (1822-1889). He did not like the notion of a wrathful God. Ritschl concluded, "The concept of God's wrath has no religious value for the Christian." So he reinterpreted the meaning of *wrath*. Wrath is the logical consequence of God's absence, and not God's attitude toward sin and evil. A lot of people liked this because it depicted a god who is above getting angry. This passive-aggressive god just gets quiet.

This god appeals to us because we have a hard time letting go of our human projections about both love and wrath. When we think of love we think of an emotion or a feeling that is often irrational. Most of the love songs we hear on the radio describe a torrent of emotions a person feels about their beloved, so much so that they would climb every mountain and swim every sea just to be with him or her. In actuality, they wouldn't. After one or two mountain ranges the emotion would begin to diminish, and the famished lover might actually prefer a cheeseburger to their beloved. After swimming just one sea (even a very small sea) I imagine the fires of love would dim.

So we hear that "God is love" and make the assumption that God is crazy in love with us. But love—particularly the wonderful Greek word *agapē*—has a different definition. To love is, in the words of Dallas Willard, "to will the good of another"; it's not primarily an emotion. Love is a desire for the well-being of another, so much so that personal sacrifice would not stand in its way. It is not that God's love is dispassionate, it's just that God's love is a lot more like a parent's love toward a child than the "love" between infatuated teens. In other words, the love of God is not an emotion that waxes and wanes.

The same is true of the word *wrath*. When we hear this word we imagine someone in a fit of rage who has lost all reason and control. Wrath is such a strong word that we use it only for extreme cases. I have seen some people get pretty *angry* and remain somewhat controlled, logical and even fair in dealing with those who have caused them to be angry. But I have no such examples for *wrath*. Wrath is a polite way of describing someone who has crossed past anger into a state of rage.

So when we speak of the wrath of God, we imagine that God is irrationally full of rage, ready to "make heads roll" because he is so livid. In the same way that God's love is not a silly, sappy feeling but rather a consistent desire for the good of his people, so also the wrath of God is not a crazed rage but rather a consistent opposition to sin and evil. God hates sin, we say (not the sinner, however), but even then, the idea of God hating something seems beneath him. We have a difficult time with the concept of God's wrath and judgment and condemnation because our only examples of these things are so negative. *+ all of Human nature*

The solution to the problem is in understanding that in the Bible the wrath of God is *pathos* and not *passion*. The *Anchor Bible Dictionary* explains the difference:

> the wrath of Yahweh is portrayed somewhat differently from human anger in the Hebrew Bible. In some respects this is essentially the difference between "passion" and "pathos." Passion can be understood as an emotional convulsion . . . and . . . a loss of self-control. . . . "Pathos" on the other hand, is an act formed with care and intention, the result of determination and decision.

The wrath of God is not like human wrath, which is a reckless and irrational passion. For example, God is never described by Paul as being angry. Anger is a human emotion. Wrath is different. God's wrath is a mindful, objective, rational response. It is actually an act of love. God is not indecisive when it comes to evil. God is fiercely and forcefully opposed to the things that destroy his precious people, which I am grateful for. It is a sign of God's love: "God's wrath must be understood in relation to his love. Wrath is not a permanent attribute of God. Whereas love and holiness are part of his essential nature, wrath is contingent upon human sin; if there were no sin there would be no wrath."

Give an example of the difference between passion and pathos. Israel pathos - 40 yrs in desert

Wrath is a necessary reaction of a loving and holy God, a good and beautiful God, to evil. God's wrath is a *temporary and just verdict on sin and evil*. As J. I. Packer notes, "God's wrath in the Bible is always judicial," and is "a right and necessary reaction to objective moral evil."

Packer concludes his point by asking, "Would a God who took as much pleasure in evil as he did in good be a good God? Would a God who did not act adversely to evil in his world be morally perfect? Surely not." And if the Creator of the universe were this indifferent, would the universe be fair? One of the things we humans cannot escape is our longing for fairness and justice. I do not want a universe in which there is no justice, no right and wrong. And I do not want a God who is indifferent to moral evil.

A GOD WHO IS MADD

I think the best example of wrath I can find on a human level is the organization known as MADD (Mothers Against Drunk Driving). This organization was created by mothers (and I assume some fathers) whose children were killed by intoxicated automobile drivers. For many years the laws against drunk driving that caused deaths were somewhat lenient, considering it involuntary manslaughter.

Often the perpetrators were not incarcerated and would drive drunk again. In response, the devastated mothers let their anger fuel their passion to work toward justice. They helped the world see that to drink until inebriated was a choice people made, and therefore these people did not kill involuntarily. Through ad campaigns and grass-roots efforts, MADD has helped toughen laws and has changed the way people think and act. In the end, it is safe to say that their efforts—while unable to bring back their own children—have saved the lives of other people's children.

These mothers' example is about as close as I can come to understanding what godly wrath looks like on the human level. God really hates the effects that sin inflicts on his children. To say that God is indifferent to child abuse or infidelity or even identity theft is ludicrous. I want no more to do with that kind of god than I do the old, vengeful god who is ready to strike me for missing my quiet time. Both are wrong. God is love, and because God is just, he stands mightily against sin and evil. And I am so glad.

HOLINESS IS THE ESSENCE OF GOD

The essence of God is holiness. Holiness is a divine attribute. God is pure. There is no sin, evil or darkness in God. The Bible proclaims the holiness of God throughout:

> Who is like you, O LORD, among the gods?
>   Who is like you, majestic in holiness,
>   awesome in splendor, doing wonders? (Exodus 15:11)

> For I am the LORD your God; sanctify yourselves therefore, and be holy, for I am holy. (Leviticus 11:44)

> And one called to another and said:
>   "Holy, holy, holy is the LORD of hosts;
>   the whole earth is full of his glory." (Isaiah 6:3)

Holiness is an essential part of God's nature. God cannot *not* be holy in the same way that God cannot *not* be love. This is not true of God's wrath, which is not an attribute of God. Wrath is not something that God *is* but something that God *does*. While it is correct to say God is holy, it is not correct to say God is wrathful. Wrath is the just act of a holy God toward sin. This is a very important distinction. Many people begin with the notion that God is angry and wrathful, but this is untrue. God is holy and pure. And God's holiness and purity are a part of God's goodness and beauty. Holiness is God's essence. God is not wrathful by nature. Wrath is what humans experience when they reject God. And it is a necessary part of God's love.

> Why is the truth that God's wrath is an action and not an attribute so important? What does the difference mean to you?

GOD DISCIPLINES HIS SONS 12:1-11 HEBREWS

OUR GOD IS A CONSUMING FIRE

For years I had trouble reconciling the love and wrath of God. A breakthrough for me came when I read the great Scottish writer and preacher George MacDonald. In one of his sermons he wrote these four profound words: "love loves unto purity." The sermon was based on the text found in Hebrews 12:29: "Our God is a consuming fire." MacDonald merged the concepts of unconditional and unending love with holiness. That is, God loves us so much that he longs for us to be pure and works tirelessly to make us pure. MacDonald points out how God is against sin and thus for humans: "He is always against sin; in so far as, and while, they and sin are one, he is against them— against their desires, their aims, their fears, and their hopes; and thus he is altogether *for them*."

God is against my sin because he is for me. And if I am for sin, God stands against those desires, MacDonald is saying, because they cause my destruction. I would not have it any other way. To be sure, I am prone to excusing my sin or rationalizing my weaknesses, but

If God's love were to "burn" something out of your life that is holding you back, what would it be?

God is not in that business. Though we are now reconciled through Christ, God is not indifferent to my sin. It hurts me, and therefore it hurts God—because God loves me.

God does not make me feel bad or shame me into better behavior. Nor does he use fear or guilt. God's method of change is the highest of all. God's holy love burns the dross of sin out of our lives. It is God's kindness that leads to genuine repentance (Romans 2:4). As MacDonald said, "love loves unto purity."

YOU DON'T REALLY WANT AN UNHOLY GOD

As I said earlier, the teddy-bear god is an appealing alternative to the "Marquis de God," the sadistic and angry god who hates and harms unjustly. But in reality, we don't want the teddy-bear god because that god is not holy. J. I. Packer asks an insightful question: "Would a God who did not care about the difference between right and wrong be a good and admirable Being? . . . Moral indifference would be an imperfection in God, not a perfection." A permissive God might say, "Sin is not such a big deal—especially if my creatures are not hurting each other. All humans sin. I'll look the other way. Sure, they are living as their own gods, but can you blame them? I made them in my image, so they're taking after me! I can overlook that too. I think they're trying to do well."

I may want this teddy-bear god when I'm feeling guilty, when my conscience is bugging me or when I want to rationalize my desire for sin. But I do not want this god in the long run. This god is like permissive parents who let their kids drink and do drugs and have sex without guilt. When we were young, we thought they were cool, but they weren't; they were lazy and did not really love their kids. Many of their kids went on to do hard drugs, and most of them wrecked their lives before they turned twenty-one. These may be the kinds of parents you think you want when you are fifteen, but you really don't.

I don't want a god who says, "It's cool. Don't sweat it. Everybody sins, just do it without the guilt, dude. Guilt stinks. Just have a good time!" This god does not love me. Being soft on sin is not loving, because sin destroys. I want a God who hates anything that hurts me. *Hate* is a strong word, but a good one. Because the true God not only hates what destroys me (sin and alienation) but also has taken steps to destroy my destroyer, I love him. And because this God destroyed sin by making the supreme sacrifice himself, taking all of the guilt and pain and suffering of my sin upon himself, I love him with an everlasting love.

THE NECESSITY OF HELL

Because God is love, hell—a place of separation from God—is necessary. Love does not demand love in return; it is not coercive. God does everything he can to reach out to us, and yet people are free to reject that love. Hell is simply isolation from God. A person—even a person others think of as decent and upright—who rejects God is experiencing hell on earth.

God will not violate the choices we make. People may choose to bar God from their life. Thus the doors of hell are locked from the inside. In John Milton's great poem *Paradise Lost*, Satan boasts, "Better to reign in hell than serve in heaven." There is a part of human life that resists relinquishing control to God. If unchecked, this resistance can lead to ruin. C. S. Lewis writes, "It is not a question of God 'sending' us to Hell. In each of us there is something growing up which will of itself *be Hell* unless it is nipped in the bud. The matter is serious: let us put ourselves in His hands at once—this very day, this hour."

God cares deeply about sin because it destroys his precious children. And God longs for holiness in us because it is the way to wholeness.

In chapters seven and eight we'll look at how our holy God makes us holy people. God willingly sacrificed himself to put an end to the problem of sin—breaking its power and taking away our guilt. Then God rose from the dead and transformed us into Christ-inhabited people who are able to triumph over temptation. In book two in The Apprentice Series, *The Good and Beautiful Life,* we'll look at how our holy God invites us into his unshakable kingdom and interacts with us in our everyday lives. *The Good and Beautiful Life* will also explore the struggles we all face (anger, lust, lying, greed, etc.) in our journey toward Christlikeness. The movement toward holiness is urged by a holy God who loves us with a holy love.

If God were unconcerned about sin, how might that harm us?

GRACE IS MORE THAN OVERLOOKING SINS

This chapter began with a story about a young woman who believed God's grace and forgiveness means he no longer cares about our behavior. A few months later I had the opportunity to talk with her about how important—and good—God's holiness is. I explained to her that God does not condone her sinful actions, but not because God is a prude.

"The reason God does not endorse what you're doing," I said, "is because you are sacred to God, and your sexuality is sacred to God. God is very 'pro-sex.' After all, it was his invention! But sexual intercourse is a sacred act of intimacy that is designed to be shared by people who have made the ultimate commitment—the covenant of marriage. Anything less than that cheapens and diminishes sex, and usually leads to a lot of pain and heartache. You are sacred and special. That's why people wait."

"I know what you mean," she said. "After a while it seemed he was only interested in me sexually, and not as a person. Our relationship is a mess. What should I do?"

"Tell him, no more until you're married."

"He'll say it's over."

"Then you'll know his true colors, and you'll be better off."

The next time I saw her, she told me that she had followed my advice, and as expected, her boyfriend did not like it, and they eventually broke up for good. However, she was smiling. She was now focusing on the sacredness of who she was. Two years later she showed up beaming outside my office. She pointed to a ring on her finger and exclaimed, "I am engaged to the most wonderful guy! He truly respects me. We decided to wait until we're married to have intercourse. Thanks for showing me who I really am."

I thought about how it had started off so badly, how I had blown it by preaching in such a way that she thought sin did not matter. Then it occurred to me that perhaps she needed first to hear that she was loved unconditionally before she could address the issue of sin. This is counterintuitive, but I believe it is right. We assume that wrath comes before grace, but that is not the biblical way. God's first and last word is always grace. Until we have been assured that we are loved and forgiven, it is impossible to address our sinfulness correctly. We will operate out of our own resources, trying to get God to like us by our own efforts to change. God's first word is always grace, as Barth said. Only then can we begin to understand God's holiness, and ours.

Margin

Dr. Richard Swenson has written a wonderful book called *Margin*. Margin refers to the space on the edge of a page where there is no text. The page you're reading has margins on the top, bottom and sides. If words stretched from top to bottom and to both edges there would be no margin. Swenson believes our lives are like that. We add so much to our schedules that we have no "margin," no space for leisure and rest and family and God and health.

Swenson describes margin and being marginless this way:

> The conditions of modern-day living devour margin. . . . Marginless is being thirty minutes late to the doctor's office because you were twenty minutes late out of the hairdresser's because you were ten minutes late dropping the children off at school because the car ran out of gas two blocks from the gas station—and you forgot your purse.
>
> Margin, on the other hand, is having breath left at the top of the staircase, money left at the end of the month, and sanity left at the end of adolescence.
>
> Marginless is the baby crying and the phone ringing at the same time; margin is Grandma taking the baby for the afternoon.
>
> Marginless is being asked to carry a load five pounds heavier than you can lift; margin is a friend to carry half the burden.

Marginless is not having time to finish the book you're reading on stress; margin is having the time to read it twice.

I think just about everyone I know can relate to this. We live in a culture that rewards busyness and overextension as signs of importance.

Swenson discovered marginlessness in the lives of his patients before he recognized it in himself. He is a medical doctor who began noticing all sorts of health hazards that were caused by stress. Stress, he discovered, came from overextension. So he started telling his patients to slow down and eliminate unnecessary things from their lives.

Then he examined his own life and discovered he was in the same condition. He realized that by working eighty-hour weeks he was compromising his health, his family time and his relationship with God. Then it hit him: those are three of his most precious resources! So he decided to cut his practice in half—which meant cutting his income in half. It wasn't easy, but according to Swenson, it was the best decision he ever made.

I've worked hard to create margin in my life, and I discovered the secret. It is simple but very difficult to do: *Just say no.*

Say no to what? Anything that is not absolutely necessary to the well-being of your soul or the welfare of others. The list of all of the activities that you feel you need to do each day or each week is probably filled with a lot of good things. This is not about good versus evil but good versus good.

Let me give an example. A young woman who was going through the material in this book was taken by the idea of margin—because she had none—so she set out to create some in her life. She had schoolwork and a job, so a set portion of her time was already spoken for. She also believed that her family time is valuable, as is prayer, Bible reading and journaling. Finally, she had a boyfriend, and she wanted to invest in their relationship. However, she realized that her boyfriend took up three to four hours of each day. She prayed about it and realized that their relationship was an area where she could create margin. She told her boyfriend that she wanted to develop their relationship, but she needed at least three nights away from him each week. This would create nine to ten hours of margin.

She later told me how meaningful this decision was. She was able to do better in school, deepen her relationship with God and her family, and go about her day with a rhythm and a pace that made her feel happy and at peace. She and her boyfriend were still able to develop their relationship as well. Remember, *God never called anyone to marginlessness.*

When we lack margin, it is our own doing and is a sure sign we have stepped outside the kingdom. So be honest and be ruthless with your schedule. Your spiritual, relational and physical health depend on it.

MARGIN AND HOLINESS

Holiness is essentially wholeness—a life that works. Sin is dysfunction or sickness. The number one spiritual sickness of our day is "hurry sickness." We are constantly in a hurry because we have overloaded our schedule. When we lack margin in our lives we become tired and lonely and joyless, which seems to invite temptation. We need margin. Margin restores balance and restores our soul, thus increasing our capacity for joy. Joy is a bulwark against temptation. Margin and holiness are related to one another in very deep ways.

Here are some ideas for finding margin:

- Get up ten minutes earlier and create a space for silence before you begin your day.

- Cut out unnecessary entertainment activities.

- Explore scaling back some of your commitments by asking, "Is it essential?" For example, must you serve on *three* church committees?

- If you do something often (for example, spending time with a friend), consider reducing the frequency without cutting that person out of your life.

FOR REFLECTION

Whether you are going through this material alone or with others, the following questions might be helpful as you reflect on your experience. Either way, it might be a good idea to answer these questions in your journal. If you are meeting with a group, bring your journal with you to help you remember your insights as you share.

1. Were you able to practice any of the suggestions for creating margin this week? If so, describe what you did and how you felt about it.

2. What, if anything, did you learn about God or yourself through the exercise?

3. As you tried to develop margin in your life, what was most difficult? What was most rewarding?

seven

God is self-sacrificing

My sister, Vicki, is an intelligent and observant person—one of the brightest people I know. She has been in the church all of her life—active in a youth group in high school, a Sunday school teacher as an adult and a member of the choir for three decades. In her lifetime she has heard hundreds of sermons. If anyone *ought* to have heard a clear message about the importance and true meaning of the incarnation, death and resurrection of Jesus, it is her. But surprisingly, she somehow managed to miss it. (Or perhaps those who stood in the pulpit failed to communicate it clearly.) She is not alone. Many people cannot give a clear and articulate explanation of why Jesus became human, died and rose again. In all honesty, the same was true of me for many years, even though I had degrees in religion. I could offer the basic explanation (Jesus died to save us from our sins) but I did not understand its inner meaning.

Vicki and her husband, Scott, took a class I was teaching on what it means to be a disciple of Jesus. A significant part of the course included deep reflection on the cross. She looked at the material we would be covering and said very honestly, "Jim, I have to admit. I've never understood the cross. It has always bothered me that Jesus had to die. And it bothered me that God would let Jesus die. It almost seems like child abuse." She went on to explain that the cross seemed unnecessary—that God could have easily "forgiven the world" simply by declaring the world forgiven, or by teaching people how to love one another. Then Jesus would not have had to suffer. There would be no need for blood.

I completely sympathized with her. The cross of Jesus, from one perspective, seems to be a dark and gruesome event. And yet, every Roman Catholic church has a crucifix—a cross with Jesus' physical body on it—and most Protestant churches have a cross on a steeple or in the sanctuary. Many of our hymns are songs of praise for the cross (for example, "When I Survey the Wondrous Cross"). The death of Jesus is front and center in Christian theology, and yet so many of us fail to grasp its significance. Understanding why Jesus chose to live among us and to die for us helped me better understand the nature of our good and beautiful God.

> Have you ever wrestled with why Jesus had to die for us? If so, explain.

FALSE NARRATIVE: WE WORK OUR WAY TO GOD

As noted in a previous chapter, we live in a performance-based world. We get what we have earned. All of the world's great religions (except Christianity) are based on this same principle. Humans must do something in order to obtain the favor and blessings of their god(s), either through worship, sacrifice, right living or all of the above. This seems logical when we reason from our own experience. The world we live in works this way: do good things, good things happen; do bad things, bad things happen. In Hinduism and Buddhism this is karma. Order your life properly, follow the precepts, offer the proper sacrifices, and God will reward you with blessing. Finding God is largely up to you. This is not only logical, it is also appealing because it allows us to remain in control.

JESUS' NARRATIVE: GOD WORKS HIS WAY TO US

The book that helped me understand why Jesus became human and had to die on the cross is *On the Incarnation*, written by Athanasius (c. 296-373), the bishop of Alexandria. Today he is credited with helping the church understand why the incarnation (God becoming human), death (the crucifixion) and resurrection of Jesus were necessary to reconcile humans to God. So after talking with Vicki about her struggle to understand why Jesus had to die, I went back to Athanasius's classic book with her questions in my mind.

I turned my questions and Athanasius's answers into a dialogue. So imagine that we have traveled back in time to ask Athanasius some hard questions about the incarnation, death and resurrection of Jesus.

JAMES: Athanasius, a common question people ask is, Why did Jesus have to become a human being and suffer and die on the cross? Why didn't Jesus just teach us about how to live in a way that is pleasing to God?

ATHANASIUS: That would have worked if mankind had not fallen into *complete corruption*. If we humans had merely broken a law we could repent of it. If our problem were ignorance, then education would be our solution. But the human problem is much deeper than that. We are corrupt and depraved. It is like a disease that cannot be cured by willpower or knowledge.

JAMES: How did we get into this predicament?

ATHANASIUS: It's a long story, but I will tell it as simply and briefly as possible. God created humans in his image, which means that they can reason and create, and they can know God. Adam and Eve were created in freedom for fellowship with God, yet they were given only one commandment with which to show their love and appreciation and obedience to God: they could not eat of the tree of the knowledge of good and evil. This tree symbolized the desire to be God, for only God truly knows good and evil. They were warned that "of the tree of the knowledge of good and evil you shall not eat, for in the day that you eat of it you shall die" (Genesis 2:17). Well, they *did* eat of this tree, and they died in a *spiritual* sense right away, cast from God's presence, no longer able to live in the easy fellowship of Eden. And consequently they began to die physically. Not only would they one day physically perish, but they were now living in the state of corruption.

JAMES: But God could have just forgiven them, right?

ATHANASIUS: No, God could not go back on his commandment. But God could also not let his precious creation be destroyed. What then was God, being good, to do? That was the divine dilemma.

JAMES: But was there no way that the humans could save themselves? Could God demand that they repent?

ATHANASIUS: No. Repentance could not change what they now were in their nature, which was corrupt. Even if they ceased from sinning—which they could not—they would still be corrupt on the inside and under the law of death.

JAMES: So, what is the solution to the problem?

ATHANASIUS: It is not what, it is rather *Who* that was needed to solve the problem. Only the Word of God himself, Who also in the beginning had made all things out of nothing, could solve the human problem. For this purpose, then, God, who is not limited by a physical body or under the power of sin, entered our world. He took to himself a body, a human body even as our own.

JAMES: But why? Couldn't God have appeared in some other form? Why did he have to have a *human* body?

ATHANASIUS: Jesus took on a body like our own because human bodies were liable to the corruption of death. He surrendered His body to death in place of all, and offered it to the Father. This He did out of sheer love for us, so that in His death all might die, and the law of death would thereby be abolished. Thus he would make death disappear as utterly as straw from fire.

JAMES: So, he took on a body so he could die? Is that right?

ATHANASIUS: Yes, corruption could not be removed other than through death. For this reason, therefore, Jesus assumed a body capable of death. It was by surrendering to death the body which He had taken, as an offering and sacrifice free from every stain, that he abolished death for His human brothers and sisters by the offering of *the equivalent*. He fulfilled in death all that was required.

JAMES: You stressed the words "offering of the equivalent." I don't understand what you mean.

ATHANASIUS: Complete corruption—which is the state of human beings after the Fall—can only be reversed by the sacrifice of complete *incorruption*. Jesus was sinless.

JAMES: What does that do for you and for me?

ATHANASIUS: Jesus reverses the original Fall by doing for us what we could not do for ourselves! By the sacrifice of His own body Jesus did two things: He put an end to the law of death which barred our way, and he made a new beginning of life for us, by giving us the hope of resurrection. Jesus, you see, destroyed death.

JAMES: Let me switch to a related topic. Why did Jesus have to die the *way* he did—on the cross? Couldn't he have died another way and still accomplished the same goal?

ATHANASIUS: Jesus had to die a very real, <u>undeniable, public</u> <u>death</u> that everyone could see. If there were no witness to His death, no one would believe His resurrection. He would be regarded as a teller of tales.

JAMES: But why did he have to die in such a shameful way? Crucifixion is the most painful and humiliating form of execution the world has ever known. Couldn't he have died a more honorable death?

ATHANASIUS: I know you abhor the cross, as you should. But note this: a marvelous and mighty paradox has occurred, for the death which they thought to inflict on Him as dishonor and disgrace has become the glorious monument of death's defeat. Though they tried to kill him in shame, the cross stands for all eternity as a symbol of the glory of God. And one final point, how could he have reached out to the entire world if He had not been crucified, for *it is only on the cross that a man dies with his arms outstretched?*

> Was there anything that Athanasius explained in the dialogue that you found helpful or that gave you a new insight?

THE RISK OF NOT BEING LOVED IN RETURN

God, who is completely free, chose willingly to enter into our world as a vulnerable child and to endure insult, torture and execution as an adult. God did not have to do this. If Athanasius is right in saying that the only way to solve the human problem (corruption, alienation from God, loss of the image of God) was by God stepping in himself, that still does not mean that God *had* to do it. There is nothing that compelled God to save us in this way. In choosing to save us in this manner God risked unrequited love. What would happen if humans rejected his love?

John tells us, "He was in the world, and the world came into being through him; yet the world did not know him. He came to what was his own, and his own people did not accept him" (John 1:10-11). This is a powerful passage because it contains several essential truths. First, "the world came into being through him." God created the world through Jesus, and Jesus continues to hold the whole world together:

> He is the image of the invisible God, the firstborn of all creation; for in him all things in heaven and on earth were created, things visible and invisible, whether thrones or dominions or rulers or powers—all things have been created through him and for him. He himself is before all things, and in him all things hold together. (Colossians 1:15-17)

Second, "he was in the world." God freely chose to enter our world, breathe our air, and subject himself to all of the pain and suffering in human life. Third, "the world did not know him." The glory of the second person of the Trinity was hidden. God did this through extreme humility. And finally, "his own people did not accept him."

Unrequited love might be the most painful of all human experiences. To love someone and not be loved in return is a deep hurt, an excruciating ache. God experienced the pain of unrequited love. Some people object to the notion that God could feel pain—or feel anything at all. Their narrative tells them that God is im-

> Have you ever felt unrequited love? Can you imagine God allowing himself to experience this pain? Explain.

passable, meaning he cannot be moved. This narrative seems to protect God's power. But if God loves others ("God so loved the world" [John 3:16]), he must also necessarily feel the pain of unrequited love. I have noticed that the people who have trouble believing God could feel pain or joy also have trouble believing Jesus could feel pain or uncertainty—or even joy. Did Jesus laugh? Did he ever feel awkward? Did Jesus ever get his feelings hurt? The Scriptures tell us that he experienced human life in its fullness, so I suspect he did.

My friend Rich Mullins once wrote a beautiful song about Jesus called "Boy Like Me/Man Like You." In it he wonders if Jesus, as a child, felt the same things we do:

> Did You grow up hungry?
> Did You grow up fast?
> Did the little girls giggle when You walked past?
> Did You wonder what it was that made them laugh? . . .
>
> Did You wrestle with a dog and lick his nose?
> Did You play beneath the spray of a water hose?
> Did You ever make angels in the winter snow? . . .
>
> Did You ever get scared playing hide and seek?
> Did You try not to cry when You scraped Your knee?
> Did You ever skip a rock across a quiet creek?

Rich told me one day that his favorite line in the song is the one about making snow angels. Why? He said, "I love the image of the One who made the actual angels as a little boy making angels in the snow."

How can self-sacrifice be a sign of strength, not weakness?

I think we have trouble with God feeling joy and pain because we think they are beneath God. Being vulnerable, we think, seems weak. But maybe not. Maybe vulnerability is true strength. Maybe sacrificing yourself for the good of another is not a sign of weakness but is the greatest power the world ever knows.

NO GREATER LOVE

The question, "Why did God do this for us when we did not deserve it?" still needs to be explored. Edward Yarnold responds: "Why did the Father will [the crucifixion]? . . . May one suggest that the answer is that human nature is made in God's own image? The law of the grain of wheat reflects God's own nature: the glory of God himself lies in self-giving. The members of Christ's body, then, share the life of the Head, who bears a crown of glory which is still a crown of thorns."

At the heart of the universe is this one principle: *self-sacrifice is the highest act*. The grain of wheat must die in order to give life. The cosmos reflects the nature of the God who created it. Jesus said, "No one has greater love than this, to lay down one's life for one's friends" (John 15:13).

Self-giving seems like a weakness. But it is an aspect of love. In 1 Corinthians 13:4-5 we read, "Love is patient; love is kind; love is not envious or boastful or arrogant or rude. It does not insist on its own way." Most of us live with the false narrative that strength is found in domination and control.

How is self-sacrifice the highest act of all?

But these are not the highest forms of power. God's power is made perfect in weakness (2 Corinthians 12:9). The power of the seed emerges only when the seed dies. The power of God is demonstrated most clearly on the cross. *To live is Christ - to die is gain*

God the Son enters our world in the lowest of all conditions, lives an utterly ordinary life for thirty years, experiences everything we experience, points the world to his Father in his teaching and in his life, and then willingly performs the ultimate sacrifice: he gives his life for all of the world, the Lamb of God taking away the world's sin. "I will sacrifice myself for your good" is the sentiment of God. And we, in our small moments of sacrifice, feel something of what God feels (freedom, release, exhilaration, purpose, meaning), if only for a few moments.

WHAT MORE COULD HE HAVE DONE FOR US?

Author and speaker Brennan Manning has an amazing story about how he got the name "Brennan." While growing up, his best friend was Ray. The two of them did everything together: bought a car together as teenagers, double-dated together, went to school together and so forth. They even enlisted in the Army together, went to boot camp together and fought on the frontlines together. One night while sitting in a foxhole, Brennan was reminiscing about the old days in Brooklyn while Ray listened and ate a chocolate bar. Suddenly a live grenade came into the foxhole. Ray looked at Brennan, smiled, dropped his chocolate bar and threw himself on the live grenade. It exploded, killing Ray, but Brennan's life was spared.

When Brennan became a priest he was instructed to take on the name of a saint. He thought of his friend, Ray Brennan. So he took on the name Brennan. Years later he went to visit Ray's mother in Brooklyn. They sat up late one night having tea when Brennan asked her, "Do you think Ray loved me?" Mrs. Brennan got up off of the couch, shook her finger in front of Brennan's face and shouted, "Jesus Christ—what more could he have done for you?!" Brennan said that at that moment he experienced an epiphany. He imagined himself standing before the cross of Jesus wondering, *Does God really love me?* and Jesus' mother Mary pointing to her son, saying, "Jesus Christ—what more could he have done for you?"

> When we talk about the power of God we often think about the mighty acts God has done, and not the incarnation and the crucifixion. Why?

The cross of Jesus is God's way of doing all he could do for us. And yet we often wonder, *Does God really love me? Am I important to God? Does God care about me?* And

Jesus' mother responds, "What more could he have done for you?" In our best moments, those times we willingly sacrifice our own needs for the good of others, we are participating, as Edward Yarnold said, in the image of God. We were made in God's image, and he willingly sacrificed himself for others. The more we come to know this God, and the more we understand our true nature, the more natural self-sacrifice will become for us.

Stories of those who sacrifice for the good of another resonate deeply with the human spirit. We see such stories in literature and film. In *The Lion, the Witch and the Wardrobe*, C. S. Lewis has Aslan, the great lion who is the Christ figure, tricking the White Witch (Satan) by offering his own life to pay the price of Edmund's transgression. The White Witch happily agrees, thinking she has defeated Aslan and his kingdom forever. But the White Witch does not know the "Deep Magic," namely, that an innocent who dies willingly for the guilty creates a force of energy more powerful than death. That is the great paradox of self-sacrifice.

> Brennan Manning admitted that he has wondered, *Does God really love me?* even though he knows the Christian story. Have you ever wondered if God really loves you? If so, what might be one way to help you find a clear answer?

THE PARADOX OF SELF-SACRIFICE

When Jesus left his heavenly throne and assumed our humanity and ultimately faced execution, he went from being the most powerful being to the weakest. Paul explains this using the beautiful words of an early Christian hymn:

> Though he was in the form of God,
>> [Jesus] did not regard equality with God

as something to be exploited,
but emptied himself,
    taking the form of a slave,
    being born in human likeness.
And being found in human form,
    he humbled himself
    and became obedient to the point of death—
even death on a cross.

Therefore God also highly exalted him
    and gave him the name
    that is above every name,
so that at the name of Jesus
    every knee should bend,
    in heaven and on earth and under the earth,
and every tongue should confess
    that Jesus Christ is Lord,
        to the glory of God the Father. (Philippians 2:6-11)

That is the paradox of self-sacrifice: by emptying and humbling himself and becoming obedient, Jesus was "highly exalted." When Jesus was asked who the greatest is in the kingdom of God, he replied, "Whoever becomes humble like this child is the greatest in the kingdom of heaven" (Matthew 18:4). The greatest are those who serve. This narrative is directly opposed to the teachings of the kingdom of this world, where the greatest are those who are *served*.

Forgiving someone makes us appear weak and vulnerable, but it actually reveals strength and

> Describe when someone made a sacrifice for your well-being. Think of a time when you sacrificed for someone else. How did you feel? Could this be a sign that you are "made in God's image"?

power. When victims forgive they become victors—not *over* others but *for* others. Our weakness prevents us from being able to forgive. Our fear keeps us from surrender and sacrifice. But people "in whom Christ dwells" learn to live and to give as Jesus did. Jesus is not merely a model to emulate or imitate, he is a source of strength to rely upon. We can do all things through Christ who strengthens us (Philippians 4:13).

HEAVEN CAME DOWN AND KISSED THE EARTH

Let's return to my sister Vicki and her question, "Why did Jesus have to die?" Jesus did not *have* to die, Jesus *chose* to die. The Father, Son and Spirit worked in harmony to reach out to a fallen and broken world in order to restore it. God did for us what we could never do for ourselves. The cross is a symbol of God's love and sacrifice. Jesus assumed and healed our human condition, and in doing so he demonstrated the depths of God's love for all of creation.

Here is a key principle of the kingdom of God: What we let go of will never be lost but becomes a thing of beauty. No wonder the manger and the cross are two of the most beautiful images this world has ever seen. In the incarnation God, who created millions of spinning galaxies, chose to become vulnerable, and in so doing, heaven came down and kissed the earth. In the crucifixion God, who could not die, subjected himself to death, and in so doing lifted the whole world to himself.

After six months of studying and reflecting on the cross, on the nature of a God who self-sacrifices, Vicki wrote me a beautiful letter explaining how she had finally, at the age of fifty-six, understood what the cross was all about. She attached the letter to a gift. I opened it and found inside a beautiful work of art in the shape of a cross, which I proudly put on my shelf in a place where I see it regularly. Every time I glance at it I give thanks to God who willingly died for us. Jesus was right when he prophesied, "And I, when I am lifted up from the earth, will draw all people to myself" (John 12:32).

Reading the Gospel of John

In *The Divine Conspiracy* Dallas Willard writes, "The key, then, to loving God is to *see Jesus*, to hold him before the mind with as much fullness and clarity as possible. It is to adore him." The best way to do this is by reading the Gospels. In the four Gospels we encounter Jesus, *seeing Jesus* in striking ways. I am always amazed at how real Jesus appears. The brilliance of these written records is in their ability to bring Jesus into vivid view.

This week I want you to find a few hours to read the entire Gospel of John. It is not often that we read an entire book of the Bible. Usually we read small portions or a short devotion based on a single verse. By reading the whole book we experience the complete story, beginning, middle and end. Some may wonder, *Why the Gospel of John, and not one of the others?* John is a unique Gospel. It begins with a prologue that tells us about the *Logos*, the Word or the Son of God, who was "made flesh, and dwelt among us." John gives us a glimpse into Jesus with a series of unique stories, but most important, John's Gospel clearly depicts Jesus' relationship with his heavenly Father.

I suggest breaking up the Gospel into four sections and reading five to seven chapters at a single sitting. I know one group took turns reading the book aloud. Watch out for the temptation to turn this into a Bible study by constantly consulting the study notes (if you have a study Bible). If you have pressing questions that arise during the reading ("Why did Jesus turn water into wine?"), you might want to write them down and search for answers at another time. For now I would like you to simply read the Gospel as if you were reading a story with a beginning, middle and end. For most people this will be a challenging exercise, but it is very rewarding.

FOR REFLECTION
Whether you are going through this material alone or with others, the following questions might be helpful as you reflect on your experience. Either way, it might be a good idea to answer these questions in your journal. If you are meeting with a group, bring your journal with you to help you remember your insights as you share your experiences.

1. Were you able to practice the exercise this week? If so, describe how you felt about it.

2. What, if anything, did you learn about God or yourself through the exercise?

3. What was your favorite passage, story or verse in the Gospel of John?

eight

God Transforms

I had not seen Carey in years when I heard that he was teaching a Sunday school class at a new church. He called and scheduled an appointment to visit me, and I was glad to see him. A successful businessman, Carey was dressed in his usual suit and tie. That made his purple WWJD? ("What would Jesus do?") bracelet stand out. After catching up I said, "To what do I owe the pleasure of this visit?" Carey's face suddenly looked sad. He had just remembered why he came.

"I really need your help," he said.

"I will if I can," I replied.

"Well, I'm really conflicted in my walk with God right now. It seems the harder I try, the worse things get. My family is fine, and my work is going well, but in my relationship with God I'm at the end of my rope."

"Usually a good place to be," I said, but he gave only a puzzled glance.

"To be specific, I'm losing the battle with sin. Big time. I travel a lot, and spend a lot of time in hotels. Pornography has become a huge temptation, and I fail every once in a while. I feel really guilty, and I tell God I'm sorry, promising never to do it again. I even confessed it to my wife, and she was pretty upset, but also understanding. She knows it isn't who I am."

I stopped him right then. "Who are you?" I asked.

"Well, I'm a Christian."

"What does that mean?" I asked.

"Well, it means that I believe in Jesus and am trying to follow his commands. I go to church, study the Bible and have devotional times when I can find an hour here or there. I try not to sin, you know; I try to be a good person, but I know that deep down I'm still just a sinner."

"I have no doubt that you're trying, Carey," I said. "And I also sense that you've been trying quite a while, with all of your effort, but it isn't helping."

"Exactly," he said. "I thought if I wore this bracelet and could keep reminding myself that I need to act like Jesus, things would improve. But they don't."

"So let me see if I have this right. You're a Christian, but you're also a sinner. Is that right?"

"Yes."

"So if you're a sinner, then what behavior would be normative for you?" I asked.

"Well, I guess sinning. But that doesn't seem right."

"And it certainly doesn't feel right, either, I suspect. The reason, Carey, that it doesn't seem right or feel right is because it isn't right. Your approach is consistently failing, right?"

"Right," he concurred.

"Maybe there's another way. I would be happy to spend some time working with you on this. But it will take some time. There is no quick fix, no magic pill. It will involve changing your mind, changing your identity and changing the way you understand what it means to live the Christian life."

"Sounds like a complete overhaul," he said.

"No, you already have all you need. You need a new approach. If you're willing to work with me on this, I think you might find there is a much better way."

"At this point I would do just about anything. Count me in," Carey said.

Carey and I met over the course of the next six months, and I began to teach him the fundamental principles found in this chapter. Carey's situation is not unlike that of many Christian men and women who are trying to change and yet fail over and over. The problem is a failure to understand the impact of the resurrected life of Jesus. In chapter seven we looked at the sacrificial, self-giving nature of the triune God, and specifically at the cross. Jesus' sacrifice was God's judgment on sin once and for all, done in order to reconcile the world to God (2 Corinthians 5:19). But the story of our good and beautiful God does not end on the cross. On the third day Jesus arose, and having defeated sin and death he now offers his life to those who follow him. The power of the resurrection is the subject of this chapter, a truth far too few Christians understand and even fewer rely on.

FALSE NARRATIVE: I AM A SINNER

Carey's story is not uncommon. All of us can relate to his struggle, though our particular temptations and sins might be different. Christians—those who have accepted Jesus as Lord and strive to follow him—find themselves in a conflict. We know that sin is wrong and would never say, "I am intending to sin today." And yet we find ourselves sinning time and again, perhaps not in the so-called big ways, but in "small" ones (white lies, coveting a neighbor's possessions, excessive worry, judging others). We are not as we ought to be.

The prevalence, and seeming dominance, of sin in our lives makes it easy to conclude, as Carey did, that our fundamental identity is "sinner." That certainly feels more realistic than "saint." Who, me? A saint? That's a joke. Our experience affirms the narrative that we are sinners, through and through. It seems most logical: I am a sinner, and that explains why I sin so much.

Great theologians, people certainly smarter than we are, have also concluded that we are fundamentally sinful. In formulating his famous slogan of the Reformation, Martin Luther said that Christians are *"simul justus et peccator,"* which means, "simultaneously *righteous* and *a sinner."* This was Luther's way of arguing against the idea that our works merit our salvation. We are saved, justified and reconciled to God—and at the same time we are sinners.

When have you heard the "I am a sinner" narrative? When have you used it?

Though the idea that Christians are sinners seems true and has been articulated by theologians past and present, I came to the conclusion that this teaching is false. It is false because it is not the narrative presented in the New Testament. It is also false because it is utterly illogical, contradictory and conflicting. As David C. Needham asks, "What could be more frustrating than being a Christian who thinks himself to be primarily a self-centered sinner, yet whose purpose in life is to produce God-centered holiness?"

That is the conflict Carey found himself in, though he did not describe it as such. He told me he was a sinner, yet he was deeply troubled by his sin. That would be like an apple tree being deeply troubled by the apples that keep growing on its branches. The teaching that we are fundamentally sinners leads to failure. I believe that most Christians have little understanding of their identity in Christ, which results in a great deal of frustration and superficial Christian living.

Carey came to me because he was frustrated by his actions. But when I looked at him I saw something else. I saw a child of God, a person in whom Christ dwells, an inhabitant of eternity bought by the blood of Christ and infused with God's power and presence, who was living a sad, fearful and defeated life. What I wanted for Carey was not simply the cessation of unwanted behavior but a deeper life in Christ—fullness, warmth, power and joy that he did not know he already possessed. In order to do that, we had to spend a lot of time studying the Bible together. His "I am a sinner" narrative was deeply embedded in his mind. Only a surplus of Scripture could help him see that his narrative was false.

NEW TESTAMENT NARRATIVE: I AM A SAINT
As we have been doing, we must replace false narratives with the narrative of Jesus. Earlier we noted that God reconciled us to himself so that we could live with him in his kingdom. This is the beginning of the process of becoming the holy people God longs for. Greg Jones describes the necessary narrative change:

> To be forgiven by God, to be initiated in the life in God's Kingdom, is to be transferred from one narrative—the narrative of death-dealing sin—to the narrative of God's reconciliation in Christ. And in that latter narrative we are forgiven of our sin so that we can learn to become holy through lifelong repentance and forgiveness.

Jones is right; our narratives must first change. The narrative of "I am an awful sinner" must be replaced by the narrative that says, "In Christ I am no longer to be defined by sin. I have been reconciled. Sin has been defeated."

Jesus not only forgives the sin of all people for all time, he broke the power of sin itself. This does not mean that everyone is saved. Only those who call upon his name experience that forgiveness.

God not only wants us to be reconciled, he wants to transform us. He not only took away the *guilt* of sin but also the *power* of sin. Those who are Christ-followers not only receive the merit of his work on the cross but actually participate, by faith, in the crucifixion. Regarding this Paul says: "We know that our old self was crucified with him so that the body of sin might be destroyed, and we might no longer be enslaved to sin" (Romans 6:6). We are not only forgiven, we have participated in Christ's death and resurrection. I am not trying to live a sinless life like Jesus. Jesus, who lived a sinless life, is now living in me.

The phrase *in Christ* or *in the Lord* occurs 164 times in Paul's epistles. Shouldn't this fact lead us to ask what it means to be "in Christ"? It gets overshadowed, I believe, by the dominant narrative that says, Jesus is over there, and sinful me is over here. The New Testament does not set Jesus apart from his followers. Rather, those who put their confidence in Jesus are also inhabited by him. Christians are people Christ dwells in.

How often have you been exposed to the message that you are "one in whom Christ dwells"?

Christians are not merely forgiven sinners but a new species: persons indwelt by Jesus, possessing the same eternal life that he has. The New Testament is unambiguous on this issue. Several Bible passages affirm this. Carefully note the language used to describe the true identity of a Christ-follower:

> To them God chose to make known how great among the Gentiles are the riches of the glory of this mystery, which is *Christ in you*, the hope of glory. (Colossians 1:27, italics added)

> When you were dead in trespasses and the uncircumcision of your flesh, God made you *alive together with him*, when he forgave us all our trespasses. (Colossians 2:13, italics added)

> I have been crucified with Christ; and it is no longer I who live, but *it is Christ who lives in me*. (Galatians 2:19-20, italics added)

> There is therefore now no condemnation for those who are *in Christ Jesus*. (Romans 8:1, italics added)

> Do you not know that *your body is a temple of the Holy Spirit* within you, which you have from God, and that you are not your own? (1 Corinthians 6:19, italics added)

But if *Christ is in you,* though the body is dead because of sin, the Spirit is life because of righteousness. (Romans 8:10, italics added)

You have died, and *your life is hidden with Christ* in God. (Colossians 3:3, italics added)

Though these are only a few of the Bible passages that describe the Christian as one who is "in Christ," they were enough to show Carey that perhaps his assumption was wrong. He said to me, "I've never even thought about Christ being in me." I have since discovered that most Christians haven't. *Really?*

WHOLE NEW CREATIONS

Once Carey saw, and was convinced, that the New Testament teaches repeatedly that Christ dwells in Christians, his next question was direct and to the point. He asked, "What does it mean to be in Christ?" To answer that, he and I began examining one verse in greater detail: "If anyone is *in Christ,* there is a *new creation:* everything old has passed away; see, everything has become new!" (2 Corinthians 5:17, italics added).

Carey raised a few question based on this passage: "How did God do this? What exactly is a 'new creation,' and what difference does that make in our lives?"

I replied, "You know how a butterfly becomes a butterfly, I'm sure. That's a pretty good analogy. The butterfly was once a caterpillar, a worm. It could only crawl, and could not fly. But it goes into a cocoon—a chrysalis, in which the root word, appropriately, is 'Christ.' And it emerges a butterfly, completely transformed. The old has passed. The new has arrived. It was once weighed down by gravity; now it can fly. Christians were once under the reign of sin, but now we can live in freedom."

"I really like that analogy, Jim," he said. "I think I understand it."

"And can you also see why it's so painful to me that so many Christians don't understand this? When I hear a Christian say, 'I'm just a sinner saved by grace,' I want to say, 'That makes as much sense as a butterfly saying, "I'm just a worm with wings."'"

We both chuckled. Then I concluded, "As a Christ-follower, you are completely reconciled to God. God is no longer dealing with you on the basis of your sin. You are forgiven forever. You're also a completely new creation—your old nature has died, and now you have been made alive with Christ. Finally, you're never going to die. Jesus defeated death by rising again, and he has imparted that new, eternal life to you. You are a completely new person who is able to experience heaven now and will be fully glorified on your final breath in this life. That seems like a good and beautiful gift, which could only come from a good and beautiful God."

Describe your level of awareness that Christ's life in you is the key to your Christian identity.

"I totally understand what you're saying. But help me understand why I still struggle with sin. Why would a butterfly want to act like a worm?" Carey asked.

SIN REMAINS BUT MUST NOT REIGN

In Christ we have been raised up with Jesus to new life. We have been given a new identity—one in which Christ dwells. We have received the indwelling Holy Spirit. We have put on Christ (Colossians 3:10). Our citizenship is now in heaven. Our spirit now cries "Abba! Father!" as a beloved child of God (Romans 8:15). However, even though we have become new people spiritually, we still live in our old self's *body*, which contains the remnants of sin. We still have our old narratives, our old memories and our old habits. We still live in a world that stands diametrically opposed to the truth of God. This is why we struggle with sin even after we're regenerated.

The Bible describes this as a conflict of the Spirit against the flesh. The word *flesh* (Greek *sarx*) refers to living apart from God. *Sarx* is what I produce when I am disconnected to God and running on my own. Paul writes, "What the flesh desires is opposed to the Spirit, and what the Spirit desires is opposed to the flesh; for these are opposed to each other, to prevent you from doing what you want" (Galatians 5:17). Paul was writing to regenerate Christians, people "in whom Christ dwells." The battle between *sarx* and Spirit does not end when we come up from the waters of baptism—in fact, that is precisely when it begins.

John Wesley, founder of the Methodist movement, states the situation this way: "Every babe in Christ is holy, and yet not altogether so. He is saved from sin; yet not entirely: It remains, though it does not reign. . . . We are 'reconciled to God through the blood of the cross.' And in that moment . . . the flesh has no more dominion over us." The Reformer John Calvin writes similarly, "For so long as we remain cooped up in this prison of our body, traces of sin will dwell in us; but if we faithfully hold fast to the promise given us by God in baptism, they shall not dominate or rule."

In this life traces of sin are still with us. We are

inseparably linked to our unredeemed flesh. Our bodies are mortal. Not just the bones and muscles, glands and senses, but mind and emotion as well. That vast, unbelievably intricate, electronic, chemical complex which is culturally, genetically, diabolically (at times), geographically, and pathologically-influenced mortality.

We do not have to be controlled by *sarx*, but we are susceptible to its demands when we are disconnected from Christ. Repeated sinful acts result from needs that long to be satisfied and cannot. We—who are no longer under sin (Romans 6:14)—nonetheless turn to sin to find what we feel is missing.

This is important because many Christians, like Carey, are stunned

---

Explain how, even though
sin remains in the Christian,
its power has been broken
and it must not reign.

---

by their capacity to sin after their conversion. While sin is not actually normative before conversion (even the unregenerate don't say about sin, "Hey, that was really life-enhancing!"), sin *after* conversion is even more disconcerting. If we are aware of and expect this conflict, it will help us deal with it; we won't be surprised. Being forewarned will help us be forearmed.

John Wesley said that in order to be on guard against sin, we must be aware that its remnants remain. The false notion that we're immune to sin, Wesley taught, "cuts off all watching against our evil nature, against the Delilah which we are told is gone, though she is still lying on our bosom. It tears away the shield of weak believers, deprives them of their faith, and so leaves them exposed to all the assaults of the world, the flesh, and the devil." Of course, the best way to prevent the temptation from defeating us is to cling to the indwelling Christ. Jesus said we need to abide in him.

A NEW WAY OF LIVING: ABIDING IN CHRIST

Because I am now a new person, a new creation, I also must live a new way. As one indwelt by Jesus, I can now live as Jesus did: in utter dependence on God, in a deep and intimate relationship with him, fully relying on God—not my willpower—to live the Christian life. Jesus used the image of a vine and its branches to describe this new way of living:

> Abide in me as I abide in you. Just as the branch cannot bear fruit by itself unless it abides in the vine, neither can you unless you abide in me. I am the vine, you are the branches. Those who abide in me and I in them bear much fruit, because apart from me you can do nothing. (John 15:4-5)

Jesus (the vine) is the life force that flows into us (the branches), thus producing fruit (love, joy, peace, etc. [Galatians 5:22]). Cut off from the vine, the branches cannot produce fruit. The power of production is not in the branch just as the power to live the Christian life is not in us. In fact, apart from Jesus, we can do nothing.

That's why Paul said, "I live; yet not I, but Christ liveth in me" (Galatians 2:20 KJV). When we separate ourselves from Christ, his life no longer flows in us, just as the branch cut off from the vine no longer has life flowing through it. But we are actual partakers and participants in the divine nature of Christ: "he has bestowed on us the precious and very great promises, so that through them you may come to share in the divine nature" (2 Peter 1:4 NAB). I am not God (or even a god), but I have been given a new nature. My faculties have been infused with Christ's life and power.

After I explained all of this, Carey asked, "So the key is to abide in Christ. How do we do this?"

I said, "To abide means to rest in and rely on Jesus, who is not outside of us, judging us, but is inside of us, empowering us. The more deeply we're aware of our identity in Christ and his presence and power with us, the more naturally we'll do this. We must get our narrative right and practice spiritual exercises to deepen our awareness of truth. In the end, Jesus' way is easy. He said that his yoke was easy and his burden was light [Matthew 11:30]. Typically, we try to do what we think Jesus wants us to do—like you did with your bracelet—by your own strength. We can't do that. But we 'can do all things through Christ who strengthens' us [Philippians 4:13]."

> How do we abide in Christ? Have you ever done this? How might it help you in the struggle with temptation?

No one has stated this truth better than James S. Stewart in his classic book *A Man in Christ*:

"Christ in me" means something quite different from the weight of an impossible ideal. . . . "Christ in me" means <u>Christ bearing me along from within, Christ the motive power that carries me on,</u> Christ giving my whole life a wonderful poise and lift, and turning every burden into wings . . . not as something you have to bear but as something by which you are borne.

COUNTRY DOGS AND CITY DOGS

Do you know the difference between country dogs and city dogs? This is a wonderful illustration about our new identity in Christ and how we go about living the Christian life. Country dogs live in wide open spaces with a great deal of freedom to roam. They can go down to the creek, wrestle with a skunk, sleep in a sunny pasture or forage for food. And at first they do. But after a while the country dog stays in the same old place, day after day: on the master's porch. The country dog has been "to Paris" as they say. He has gotten into a few scrapes and has seen the open range for what it is. Now, the country dog is content to stay near the master. After all, he may get a biscuit or a pat on the head or a belly rub.

The city dog is quite different. The city dog lives cooped up in a house and is forbidden to leave the home. The city dog has one aim: getting out! The city dog has learned when and how the doors will be opened, and how to nudge it just so in the hope of escape. The moment the door is cracked open, the city dog makes a run for it. The master may have to run after the dog or even get in the car and search the neighborhood for the fugitive, constantly yelling the dog's name, begging it to come home. If the master sees the dog, he or she will likely have to bribe the dog with a biscuit or lasso the dog with a leash in order to get it home.

Those who approach the Christian life with a set of rules and laws and dos and don'ts are like the city dog. My experience is that many Christians feel cramped and confined, and would love to escape their rules. I know I did. Those who understand their identity in Christ are like the country dog. They know that they are not under the law, and they know that they can sin, but having sinned before, they know better. They are more content living close to the master. An Orthodox writer puts it this way: "The spiritual life is not a life of laws and precepts but a life of participation, affection and love, a life mingled and mixing with God."

MEANT TO HOUSE THE FULLNESS OF GOD

What I said earlier may have sounded shocking to some: Christians "can sin." This does not mean that they ought to sin. We were not made for sin; we have died to it. But we certainly can and do sin. As Christians we are not under the law (Romans 6:14). No set of rules or lists of dos and don'ts define a Christian. And guilt is an ineffective motivator over time. But that does not mean we can do whatever we want, as Paul explains: " 'All things are lawful for me,' but not all things are beneficial. 'All things are lawful for me,' but I will not be dominated by anything" (1 Corinthians 6:12).

I am free to make choices about what I do and do not do. But pay attention to this: *Those choices should be made in light of who I am, not to determine who I am.* I am one in whom Christ dwells, and that should guide my decisions. Will this activity be beneficial to me? Will that activity enslave me? These are the questions we now ask. We are now led by the Spirit, which is the secret to holiness. Understanding our true identity and acting from that is a much stronger motivator than guilt.

> Which of the metaphors for our relationship with Christ (vine and branches, temples in whom the Spirit dwells, butterflies, or country dogs) best explains the concept of abiding in Christ and encourages you the most?

I said to Carey at this point, "Was watching that garbage on the television truly compatible with who you are?"

"No. Before, when I thought I was a corrupt sinner, the answer was yes. What I see now is that the person who thinks they're a sinner may turn the TV off, but with some regret and with a desire to turn it back on. The person who knows who they are in Christ can learn to turn it off without any lingering desire."

At that moment I knew he was getting it.

One of my favorite stories is about John of Kronstadt. He was a nineteenth-century Russian Orthodox priest at a time when alcohol abuse was rampant. None of the priests ventured out of their churches to help the people. They waited for people to come to them. John, compelled by love, went out into the streets. People said he would lift the hungover, foul-smelling people from the gutter, cradle them in his arms and say to them, "This is beneath your dignity. You were meant to house the fullness of God." I love that phrase: *you were meant to house the fullness of God.* That describes you and me. Knowing that this is our true identity is the secret to walking in holiness.

GOD'S POWER IN OUR BROKENNESS

Like John of Kronstadt, we can say to the broken, "Your brokenness does not define you." You are one in whom Christ dwells. You were meant to house the fullness of God. We welcome them like the prodigal son, restoring them to their true birthright, even if they have trouble accepting it. But we offer the same message to people like Carey—the good and upright "elder brothers," the ones who try so hard and fail. To those who struggle to be perfect, who live with a deep sense of failure and self-hatred, the message is the same: You are one in whom Christ dwells. Your glory is not in what you do, but in who you are. — *Christ — the great enabler*

Both the wounded and the legalists need to hear an even deeper paradox. It is in our weakness that God's power is revealed. The broken feel they have nothing to offer; legalists feel their perfection is what makes them valuable. Both are wrong. We minister out of our brokenness. We heal others through our vulnerability because that is where Christ shines most brightly. Then we can offer them the one thing people most need: Jesus. Henri Nouwen writes:

> The question is not: How many people take you seriously? How much are you going to accomplish? Can you show some results? But: Are you in love with Jesus? . . . In our world of loneliness and despair, there is an enormous need for men and women who know the heart of God; a heart that forgives, cares, reaches out and wants to heal.

I shared with Carey the truth that God's power is made perfect not in perfection (which is an illusion and a delusion) but in weakness (2 Corinthians 12:9). I encouraged him to trust that others want to know and experience the Christ that he knows, the One he discovered when he quit trying to earn his acceptance and simply received it.

My friend and colleague Patrick Sehl is director of campus ministries at Friends University, where I teach. Patrick is a master of visual illustrations. Wanting to communicate the paradox of how we minister to others through our brokenness, he took a cardboard box and asked his students to "beat it up." They punctured holes in the box, kicked it around and tore pieces off of it. Then he placed the box on a table in front of them all. Underneath the box was a light. He dimmed the house lights, and then turned on the light inside the box. He didn't need to say any more. They all understood. The light of Jesus shines clearly through our broken places.

In your own life, have you experienced the paradox that weakness and vulnerability allow Christ to shine most clearly? Or have you experienced it through the life of someone you know? Explain.

GIVING WHAT WE HAVE: THE CHRIST IN US

The New Testament approaches the Christian life by telling us who we are and whose we are, and then it encourages us to live in a manner worthy of that identity. Carey was able to understand this, and his life changed accordingly. His particular struggle was with lust, and I talked more specifically with him about that temptation—where it comes from and how it can be dealt with. But the same process works for any of our besetting sins. The second book in this series, *The Good and Beautiful Life,* looks specifically at those struggles, dealing head-on with anger, lust, lying, greed, worry and the like. But no matter what the vice, our identity in Christ is the foundation for dealing with them. It takes time to understand this. Old narratives are hard to change. *The best approach is to keep soaking in the truth of our identity in Christ, practicing spiritual disciplines that deepen those truths and being part of a community that will reinforce those truths.*

Carey came to see me a few years later. His smile never left during our conversation. He said, "I think the day I got it was when I was preparing for a trip out of town. I used to get nervous, and I would pray, 'Lord, I don't want to fail you again.' But this time I had no anxiety. When I got to the hotel room, I walked to the television, closed the doors of the console and smiled. I whispered to myself, 'I know who I am. I am a child of God. I house the fullness of God.' I was never tempted to turn the TV on, even to watch the news. I'm not prideful. I know that sin remains, as you taught me. But it doesn't reign anymore. I used my free time to read and to rest. I knew I *could* sin, and I knew that God would still love me. But I didn't *want* to sin. That's when I knew it had finally taken root in me. I never knew it could be this easy."

He continued, "And best of all, I got the courage to share my story with some other people. I was afraid at first that I would be judged. But that's not what happened. Instead, a lot of people came to me and asked if I would help them. Not long afterward, I started an accountability group for guys who struggle with lust. We meet weekly to encourage each other. We remind each other who we are. The changes I've seen are dramatic."

God is in the business of changing names. Abram to Abraham. Saul to Paul. And he changes your name and mine: from sinner to saint, from being a person living in isolation to a person in whom Christ dwells. He takes that which is broken and mends it by his grace. And he reaches out to others through those places where his grace is most visible in us.

solitude

The central aim of this chapter has been to help you understand who you are. Christians are those in whom Christ dwells. But since it's likely that we have built our sense of self on wrong core narratives ("I am really good," "I am really bad," "I am pretty" or "I am fat"), we need to engage in an activity that will help us experience this new core narrative: solitude.

Solitude is spending time apart from other people. Usually we experience solitude when no one happens to be around. But that's not the kind of solitude I'm describing. Effective solitude is intentional time alone with ourselves and with God. Then God can do something powerful within us in the area of identity. Dallas Willard observes:

> When we go into solitude and silence, we stop making demands on God. It is enough that God is God and we are his. We learn we have a soul, that God is here, and this world is "my Father's house." This knowledge of God progressively replaces the rabid busyness and self-importance that drives most human beings, including the religious ones.

When we step away from people for a period of time, there is no one to impress, no one's opinions of us, no image to live up to or down to. Let me give an example. For a few years I would make occasional trips to a nearby retreat house for a half day of solitude, rest and prayer. A sign above a desk in the house read:

Welcome to this place of solitude
Feel free to take off your masks

Because there was no one around, I could be myself. There was no need to be clever or funny or smart. And after I came face to face with myself, I encountered God. And God—not the world, not my friends or family members—began to shape my identity.

A WORD TO EXTROVERTS

Some of us undoubtedly will feel anxious about seeking solitude. A friend and colleague I mentioned earlier, Patrick Sehl, said to me, "Of all of the exercises you've taught me over the years, this one is the hardest for me." Patrick is an extrovert; he loves to be with people and doesn't like to be alone. He also, by his admission, struggles with attention deficit—his mind runs all over the place. As long as he is with other people or working on projects, his mind stays focused. But when in solitude, his thought life spins out of control. Over the years I've learned that people like Patrick are in the majority.

For introverts—people who find great peace and comfort in solitude—being alone for an hour or two is a joy. One woman in a class I taught said, "Is that all—one to two hours? I usually need five hours of solitude to really connect with God." Personality type and individual temperament play a significant role in solitude, perhaps more than for any other spiritual exercise.

> "We need to find God, and he cannot be found in noise and restlessness. God is the friend of silence. . . . We need silence to be able to touch souls. The essential thing is not what we say, but what God says to us and through us."
>
> MALCOLM MUGGERIDGE

This does not mean that extroverts should try to avoid solitude. Quite the opposite. The difference is in the approach. If you're like Patrick, give yourself a lot of grace in the beginning. Start with only five to ten minutes at a time. Grab a cup of something good to drink, take a seat and relax, be still for as long as you're able. While you're experiencing solitude, feel free to have background music playing or to have a simple task to keep you focused, like doing the laundry, ironing or washing the dishes. Do not be legalistic about this. If you get uncomfortable, say a prayer of thanks and go back to whatever you were previously doing. The aim is to help you learn how to be more comfortable alone with yourself and God.

YOUR IDENTITY IN CHRIST

During your time of solitude you might want to read the following verses about our identity in Christ. Read a verse slowly and spend a few minutes reflecting on it. Don't rush or try to accomplish anything. Just allow your mind to dwell on the truths of the Bible regarding your true identity. This will focus your thoughts and deepen the truths discussed in this chapter.

- I am God's child: "But to all who received him, who believed in his name, he gave power to become children of God." (John 1:12)

- I have been justified, and have peace with God: "Therefore, since we are justified by faith, we have peace with God through our Lord Jesus Christ." (Romans 5:1)

- I am free from condemnation: "There is therefore now no condemnation for those who are in Christ Jesus." (Romans 8:1)

- I am alive together with Jesus: "And when you were dead in trespasses and the uncircumcision of your flesh, God made you alive together with him, when he forgave us all our trespasses." (Colossians 2:13)

- I cannot be separated from God's love: "For I am convinced that neither death, nor life, nor angels, nor rulers, nor things present, nor things to come, nor powers, nor height, nor depth, nor anything else in all creation, will be able to separate us from the love of God in Christ Jesus our Lord." (Romans 8:38-39)

- I am seated with Christ in the heavenly realm: "God . . . raised us up with him and seated us with him in the heavenly places in Christ Jesus." (Ephesians 2:4, 6)

- I am in the Spirit, not the flesh: "But you are not in the flesh; you are in the Spirit." (Romans 8:9)

- Jesus is my life: "When Christ who is your life is revealed, then you also will be revealed with him in glory." (Colossians 3:4)

- I am being transformed into the image of Christ: "And all of us, with unveiled faces, seeing the glory of the Lord as though reflected in a mirror, are being transformed into the same image from one degree of glory to another; for this comes from the Lord, the Spirit." (2 Corinthians 3:18)

FOR REFLECTION

Whether you are going through this material alone or with others, the following questions might be helpful as you reflect on your experience. Either way, it might be a good idea to answer these questions in your journal. If you are meeting with a group, bring your journal with you to help you remember your insights as you share your experiences.

1. Were you able to practice the exercise this week? If so, describe what you did and how you felt about it.

2. What, if anything, did you learn about God or yourself through the exercise?

3. Solitude allows us to grow in the ability to "take off our masks" and simply be who we truly are in the presence of God. Would that describe your experience with this exercise? Explain.

nine

HOW TO MAKE A PICKLE

One evening my son, Jacob, and I decided to attend a concert at church. We left our house early so we could stop at a local coffee shop to get a soda for him and a cup of coffee for me. Over the previous few months I had been thinking about the need to slow down to savor life's moments, so I was pleased that we had created some margin to spend a few moments together—rather than rushing, as usual.

Once we sat down with our drinks I settled in, enjoying the present moment. But Jacob chugged down his soda, began fidgeting and with typical adolescent impatience said, "C'mon, Dad, let's go."

"But we've got fifteen minutes."

"Then let's go . . . somewhere else," he pleaded.

"Why? I want to relax and enjoy my coffee."

"C'mon, please. This is boring."

I had been thinking a lot about American "hurry sickness," always being in a rush, and the causes behind it. Hurriedness is an inner attitude that is not necessarily caused by outer circumstances; boredom is one of its symptoms. The solution to the problem is counterintuitive: being present where you are.

"I'll make you a deal," I said. "We can go as soon as you notice five things about this place that you've never noticed before." He had been in that same coffee shop a half dozen times before.

"What do you mean?" he asked.

"Look around the room. Look at the walls, the ceilings, and spy five things you've never really paid attention to before."

He looked up at the ceiling. "Well, I never noticed that yellow thing," he said, pointing to the awning.

"Good," I said. "Keep going."

He looked around. "There's an apron pinned to the wall over there. Never noticed that before. Oh, and there's a picture of a dog on the other wall."

"Three down, two to go."

"Um, well . . . those lamps, the brown ones—I never noticed them. And . . . the floor, it has gray and black tiles. I've never looked at them either."

"You did it!" I said.

But here was the amazing thing. Instead of wanting to leave right away, he kept looking around. His anxious face now looked peaceful, even interested. Maybe it was the fact that I had turned it into a game, but maybe not. Maybe he was actually discovering something that had been right under his nose the whole time.

"Okay, Jake. You know your weird dad is always trying to teach you something. What's the point of this little exercise?"

He paused for a few seconds and then said, "Stop and notice the world's features."

"Brilliant!" I responded. "Why is that important?"

"I guess because the world has a lot of things worth noticing."

More wisdom! I was so proud of my boy.

"That's right," I said. "And I also wanted to show you what I've been learning for the past few months. You see, we get anxious and say we're bored, but what's really happening is that we aren't paying attention; we aren't living in the present moment. And we do that because we think the present moment isn't interesting. But it is! You just discovered that if you stop and notice the world's features you can stop feeling bored and start enjoying life."

"Yeah, I get it, Dad. Can we go now?"

Okay. So we learn slowly. But at least it was a start.

FALSE NARRATIVE: MARTHA'S WAY IS BEST

Jesus did not have a lot to say specifically about hurry, busyness and distraction, but there is one narrative in the Gospels that deals directly with these problems: the story of the sisters Martha and Mary. They lived in Bethany with their brother, Lazarus, and apparently Jesus stayed with them when he was in town. When Jesus and his disciples came for dinner, Martha began to panic. She had too much to do and not enough time to do it—a recipe for hurry. Her sister chose not to help with the preparations but instead sat at the feet of Jesus and listened to his teaching. Martha confronted Mary about this and asked Jesus to scold Mary for not helping her: "*Martha was distracted by her many tasks;* so she came to him and asked, 'Lord, do you not care that my sister has left me to do all the work by myself? Tell her then to help me' " (Luke 10:40, italics added).

Being overcommitted, too busy and preoccupied are not new to contemporary society. Martha was confronted with the same dilemma we face every day. Will we take on too many things or be concerned about the wrong things and thus miss the most important things?

THE NEED FOR SPEED

Hurry and distraction are nothing new, but in our age we seem to have perfected them. More than at any time in history, we have become obsessed with productivity, speed and efficiency. Economist and writer Jeremy Rifkin notes:

> We are a nation in love with speed. We drive fast, eat fast, make love fast. We are obsessed with breaking records and shorten-

ing time spans. We digest our life, condense our experiences, and compress our thoughts. We are a culture surrounded by memos and commercials. While other cultures might believe haste makes waste, we are convinced that speed reflects alertness, power, and success. Americans are always in a hurry.

I believe he's right. And while we increasingly move faster, we are enjoying life less.

Speed can be wonderful. I love the Internet's speed. The fact that I can leave my home in the morning and be in Los Angeles in time for lunch is wonderful. No, speed is not the problem. Our love of it is. Our impatience has made life a dizzying blur. And as a result, our spiritual lives are diminished. As we try harder, we are becoming spiritually shallow and deeply disappointed—not exactly a recipe for a robust life.

> What is the correlation between being in a hurry, noticing things around you and contentment?

Once again, Jeremy Rifkin puts his finger on our problem:

> It is ironic that in a culture so committed to saving time we feel increasingly deprived of the very thing we value. . . . Despite our alleged efficiency . . . we seem to have less time for ourselves and far less time for each other. . . . We have quickened the pace of life only to become less patient. We have become more organized but less spontaneous, less joyful. We are better prepared to act on the future but less able to enjoy the present and reflect on the past. . . . Today we have surrounded ourselves with time-saving technological gadgetry, only to be overwhelmed by plans that cannot be carried out, appointments that cannot be honored, schedules that cannot be fulfilled, and deadlines that cannot be met.

How did we get into this predicament?

MONKS AND CLOCKS

The clock was invented by monks. Apparently they had a lot of time on their hands (pun intended). They invented the clock because they wanted to regulate their times of prayer and labor. The Rule of St. Benedict, written in the sixth century, includes these words: "Idleness is the enemy of the soul, therefore all the community must be occupied at definite times in manual labor and at other times in *lectio divina.*"

According to Benedict, there are two activities that elevate the soul—working and praying. And they certainly do. The clock allowed the monks to precisely regulate their daily activities. Each day a monk would watch the clock and ring the bell at the appointed hours for work and prayer.

The notion that "idleness is the enemy of the soul" became pervasive in the monasteries. The monks felt that hard work was a way to serve God. But though they worked hard, they also spent four to five hours a day reading and praying, which go a long way toward eliminating stress. They had the clock, but they did not have hurry sickness. In a few centuries that would begin to change, and during the twentieth century hurry sickness would become the number one spiritual illness of our day.

In 1370 a public clock was erected in Cologne, Germany. The city passed an ordinance establishing the hours of the work day and setting curfews for the first time. Thus, clock time began "gaining the upper hand over Natural Time." Natural time is organic: light and dark; winter, spring, summer and fall; sun and moon mark time's passage. The clock on the other hand is an artificial measurement of time, breaking natural time into seconds, minutes and hours.

Monks invented the clock, but we cannot blame them for our obsession with speed. Technology is at fault. With the invention of the machine a whole new approach to work and productivity emerged. The machine is the model of efficiency: it works ceaselessly and tirelessly until it breaks down. We created machines ostensibly to help us become better workers and more productive, but there were also unintended consequences. We "invented the machine and then took it as its life model."

Instead of seeing ourselves as organisms—flexible and fluid, designed for rest and recreation, laughter and learning—we came to see the human person as yet another machine. The more machine-like I am, the better. Contemplation and leisure became less important. Then Frederick Wilson Taylor changed the narrative even further.

What is the connection between technology and hurry sickness?

In the first decade of the twentieth century Taylor took a stopwatch to the Midvale Steel plant in Philadelphia. With the owner's approval, Taylor broke down every job into a series of tasks and timed workers as they performed those tasks. He then tried to find ways to perform the tasks more efficiently—he called it "the system." The workers hated the system but productivity soared. Taylor wrote these chilling words in his 1911 treatise *The Principles of Scientific Management*. "In the past, man has been first, in the future the system must be first." → SAD)

THE TYRANNY OF THE URGENT—EVEN IN OUR CHURCHES

Taylor was right about the future; the "system" certainly is first. We have unhesitatingly bowed to the god of productivity and sacrificed our wellness in order to appease it. "'Taylor's system' is still very much with us; it remains the ethic of industrial manufacturing." Tonight I went inside a fast-food restaurant instead of going through the drive-through window. Why? The line was too long at the drive-through. I wanted my fast food fast. As I impatiently waited for my food, I noticed a digital sign behind the counter. It read: "AVG SERVICE TIME: 45 SECONDS."

The manager barked out commands to every person on the assembly line, imploring them to hurry up. The reason? Her salary is dependent on that average service time. The restaurant is built on the dominant narrative of Frederick Taylor. Ben Franklin's adage "time is money" is also a part of the false narrative. Time, of course, is *not* money. The narrative behind Franklin's quote is that productivity determines value. As a result, we live under the "tyranny of the urgent." This gives birth to the modern obsession with multitasking, doing more than one thing at a time.

The mantra of our achievement-oriented world is, "You are only as valuable as what you produce." This leads to the narrative that what we produce determines our value, and therefore the more we produce the more valuable we are. What we did yesterday is old news; what matters is what we are doing today.

> Do you live under the tyranny of the urgent? Why or why not?

I recently read about a new phenomenon called "omni-tasking." Omni-taskers believe that they can do more than a few things at once; they do nearly *everything* at once! We are guilty of this problem in our churches. Many Christians attribute their lack of margin to being overtasked by their churches. With a slight twist, churches sometimes operate under the Fred Taylor narrative: *the church (not the system) is more important than the person.* I know a half dozen committed Christian women and men who burned out by being overextended by their churches. Because they did things well, they were asked to be on more church committees and to help with more church programs. They became so busy that they finally collapsed.

Satan does not always appear as a red devil, a ghastly monster or the object of sexual desire. Sometimes he simply inserts a false narrative (achievement equals value) into our minds. Once that narrative gets firmly planted, we are headed toward destruction without realizing it. The narrative can sound almost Christian. That's why it slips in unnoticed. We may even think we're doing pretty well. But one day we wake up and realize that the things most important to us—time with God and our family, our emotional and physical health—were sacrificed on the altar of achievement (or the success of our church). And we have nothing to show for such an amazing sacrifice.

Like most false narratives, this particular one contains a measure of truth. Certainly it is good to be productive and to do things well. The Bible is full of admonitions to work diligently. And when people seek membership in a church, they pledge to serve it with their prayers, their presence, their gifts and their service. But we can be sure God does not call us to be overcommitted. We do it to ourselves by following the dominant narrative that success and achievement are more important than the well-being of our souls.

REALLY BAD PROPHETS

In 1967, futurists told a Senate subcommittee that by 1985, thanks to technological advances, Americans would be working twenty-two hours a week for twenty-seven weeks a year. The average worker would retire at age thirty-eight! *They predicted we would have too much time on our hands.* The reality is that since 1973 leisure time in America has *decreased* 37 percent. How is this possible?

No one can save time; we can only spend it. We cannot put time in a bottle and use it later. Technology does reduce the time we have to

Give some examples of how technology has actually decreased your leisure time.

spend on certain tasks. Thanks to the microwave I can bake a potato much faster than I could using a conventional oven. Editing an essay on a computer is quicker than retyping it on my typewriter. Email allows me to contact a friend in England in a matter of seconds, whereas "snail mail" would take weeks to reach him.

So, where did the "extra" (not saved) time go? We use it on other things. All of these technological advances have *raised the expectations* of what we can get done, so we added more onto our schedule. We increase our workload to keep up with or get ahead of others. If we fail to raise the bar, we will fall behind, be less productive and thus feel less important.

HOW OUR LIGHT IS SPENT

The great poet John Milton gave us the phrase, "When I consider how my light is spent." The elderly Milton wrote those words as he was going blind. He looked back on his life and pondered how he spent his time, his light, while he had it. Let's examine how we spend our time. In a lifetime today's average person spends

- six months sitting at traffic lights
- eight months opening junk mail
- one year searching through desk clutter
- two years trying to call people who are not in
- three years in meetings
- five years waiting in lines

In a single day an average American will

- commute forty-five minutes
- be interrupted seventy-three times
- receive six hundred advertising messages
- watch four hours of television

No wonder we have the attention span of a ferret on a triple cappuccino. And what do we have to show for all of this added "productivity"? Health-related problems are skyrocketing and families spend less time together. In fact, the average working parent spends twice as long dealing with e-mail as playing with his or her children. In his excellent book *In Praise of Slowness* Carl Honoré tells how the book

titled *One-Minute Bedtime Stories* came to be: "To help parents deal
with time-consuming tots, various authors have condensed classic
fairy tales into sixty-second sound bites."

SOME THINGS CANNOT BE RUSHED

The most important aspects of our lives cannot be rushed. We cannot
love, think, eat, laugh or pray in a hurry. Someone once said to me,
"You know to spell love? T-I-M-E." My children want my time more
than anything else. My daughter, Hope, tells me that her favorite days
are those we keep the sabbath in our home. We build forts, eat ice
cream and play games. I play the guitar, and she loves it (no matter
how often I miss a note, which is often). We cook meals together—no
fast food! Giving her my time says "I love you. You are important."

Taking time is especially important in our spiritual lives. *In our
spiritual life we cannot do anything important in a hurry.*

When we are in a hurry—which comes from overextension—we
find ourselves unable to live with awareness and kindness. Fortunately, God never calls us, as Richard Foster likes to say, "into a life
of panting feverishness." If we are overcommitted and in a hurry, we
may feel like we're being especially effective and that God is therefore proud of us. God knows quite well that our distracted and en-
cumbered lives pull us away from the one thing we need the most.

JESUS' NARRATIVE: MARY'S WAY IS BETTER

Let's go back to the story of Martha and Mary to see what Jesus might
have to say about our panting feverishness. After Martha asked Jesus
to admonish Mary for not helping with the chores, Jesus gently rebuked Martha: "Martha, Martha, you are worried and distracted by
many things; *there is need of only one thing.* Mary has chosen the better part, which will not be taken away from her" (Luke 10:41-42,
italics added).

I say Jesus *gently* rebuked Martha because Jesus said her name
twice, "Martha, Martha." He does this because she doesn't deserve

harsh criticism. Martha means well. She is trying to serve her guests.

Most of us do not need to eliminate bad things from our lives in order to slow down and find balance: *Which should I keep? Bible reading or recreational drug use?* We must choose between multiple good activities. We simply do not have enough time to do all that we would like to do. When we add too many things to our lives, something has to be eliminated. Unfortunately, busy people often rid themselves of the most important ones: relationships, spiritual practices and self-care (for example, eating right and exercising).

Jesus told Martha, "There is need of only one thing." That one thing is listening to Jesus. Jesus did not say that the "one thing" was to obey his commandments (though that will come). The first thing, the one needful thing, is to listen to his teachings. The world tries to pull us away from this important thing. Martha's way was good, but Mary's way was better. She looked at the situation and evaluated what was most important. Jesus was in her home, and being with him was the most important thing she could do.

Remember George Herbert's poem (see pp. 103-4)? The soul says to God, "My dear, then I will serve." And God responds, "You must sit down and taste my meat." Martha was driven and distracted by the need to serve. In itself, service is not a bad thing, but it's not always the best thing. At that time, on that day, the best thing Mary could have done was to sit at the feet of Jesus and listen. Too many of us are trying to serve God without listening to God. There will be time to serve, but listening to Jesus always takes precedence.

THE RHYTHM OF JESUS

Jesus gives us the best example of a well-paced life. In the Gospels we see Jesus retreating to be alone (nine times in the Gospel of Luke alone). Jesus lives his life in perfect rhythm, the proper tempo, at all times. He will not be rushed. He never does anything in haste.

I love this passage in Mark's Gospel:

> In the morning, while it was still very dark, he got up and went
> out to a deserted place, and there he prayed. And Simon and his
> companions hunted for him. When they found him, they said
> to him, "Everyone is searching for you." He answered, "Let us
> go on to the neighboring towns, so that I may proclaim the
> message there also; for that is what I came out to do." And he
> went throughout Galilee, proclaiming the message in their syn-
> agogues and casting out demons. (Mark 1:35-39)

Notice the balance of contemplation and action, or, in the words of
John Wesley, "piety and mercy." Before dawn Jesus goes off to a quiet
place to pray. He spends time alone with his heavenly Abba.

But his disciples panic when they discover Jesus is missing, especially in light of all the work that must be done. "Where have you
been?" asks Peter. Jesus simply responds, "Let's go." Without
hesitation he proclaims the good news of the available kingdom,
and demonstrates its power through signs and wonders. See
the perfect balance? He rests and recreates, yet he also works and serves.

Jesus lived a perfect life of balance between rest and action. Describe your "balance."

Jesus' identity was deepened in periods of silence and solitude, in
time alone with his heavenly Father. That was his secret to balancing
contemplation and action, rest and labor. He knew who he was. And
for those of us "in whom Christ dwells," the rhythm should be the
same. As we spend time in quiet and rest and contemplation, sitting
at the feet of Jesus, we gain strength to act in wisdom in the hustle
and bustle of a busy world. In slowing down we can hear the Spirit
whisper that we are loved, and then we begin to reflect the glory of
the Christ who is within us. We become the kind of people this fraz-
zled and frightened world most needs.

RUTHLESSLY ELIMINATE HURRY

When my friend John Ortberg took on a new and very demanding role in ministry, he called Dallas Willard for advice. With pen and notepad in hand, John was ready to write down a half dozen or more key things. Dallas began by saying, "Ruthlessly eliminate hurry from your life." John wrote it down.

"Okay. What's next?" queried John.

"There is no next. Just do that, John, and you'll be fine."

Dallas knew that John already had everything he needed to be effective in this new role. John is one of the most brilliant and most deeply committed Christ-followers I have ever met. He has a great grasp of the Bible, a thorough understanding of theology and ministry, years of practice in spiritual formation, and the Holy Spirit as his guide. John did not need any new insights or techniques. But he needed to overcome the number one enemy in the spiritual life: hurry sickness.

Why is eliminating hurry from our lives so crucial? When we eliminate hurry we become present, or more specifically, present to the present moment in all of its glory. We become aware of our surroundings. We see colors and smell smells; we hear hushed sounds and can actually feel the wind in our faces. In short, we "show up" and experience the fullness of life. And that includes, not least of all, being present to God. If I am to live well as a Christian, I need to be constantly connected to God. Hurry is not part of a well-lived life.

It is possible to act quickly without hurrying. If I have only ten minutes to get from one end of the airport to another, I can move quickly without hurrying. Hurry is an inner condition that is fear-based: "If I don't make my plane everything will be ruined. Life as I know it is over!" But when I walk in step with God I learn to say, "If I don't make that plane I'll be fine. God is with me. Things will work out. Meanwhile, I'll move my legs as fast as I can while my heart is happy and unhurried."

"Hurry," said Carl Jung, "is not *of* the Devil; it *is* the Devil." When hurried, we cannot experience life at its fullest; nor can we come into contact with our true selves, our real feelings. And even more important, we outrun God. When we slow down we allow ourselves to be found, found by life and found by God. When we practice slowing down, we are moving into the rhythm of God. When we eliminate hurry (our part, in response to God's gracious call to the deeper life), the Spirit comes alongside us and strengthens us.

THE KINGDOM IN MY BACKYARD

One day, in the midst of my effort to slow down and become present, I decided to take an afternoon to try to live "deliberately," as Henry David Thoreau put it. It was an unseasonably warm mid-February day, so I sat in an Adirondack chair in my backyard. Of course, the leaves had long ago fallen, but one bushy tree really stood out. Normally, I would never have paid much attention to this tree, and given the time of year I would not have spent more than a few minutes in the backyard. But there it was, and it had my full attention.

After a few minutes I noticed something strange about this tree in addition to its leaves: it had lots of tiny grape-like berries. I began to wonder why it was full of berries at this time of the year. Because I had been in and out of prayer that afternoon, I turned my attention to God and asked, "God, why is this tree full of berries?" Right on cue a little bird, the size of a finch, flew to the tree, skewered a berry and flew to a nearby bush where it dined. The Spirit whispered, "*That is why the tree is full of berries.*"

It was as if the Sermon on the Mount was being preached in my backyard. "Look at the birds of the air and how they neither sow nor reap but are fed by their Father in the heavens" (see Matthew 6:26). But the sermon was not over. The Spirit then led me to consider just how many berries were on that tree. There were thousands. And then I was led to consider how small those little birds are, so small they could fit in the palm of my hand. The point: God has provided more for them than they will ever need. The application: when we live with the good and beautiful God, we have access to more than we will ever need.

It was a powerful sermon that I would have missed had I not been "foolish" enough to step off the achievement treadmill and plant myself in the middle of my backyard for an hour. Robin Myers writes, "In every waking hour a sacred theater is in session, played out before an audience that is largely blind." I want to see this sacred theater every day of my life. I don't want to miss all that God has in store.

> Have you ever had an experience like the berry-filled tree, where you stopped and paid attention to your surroundings and discovered something wonderful? Describe that experience.

This treasure is only found in the present moment. As authors Richard Bailey and Joseph Carlson explain, "Life is really nothing more than a series of present moments—one right after the other— to be experienced. . . . You are always living in this moment: will you live it present or absent?" I want to be present. (Isn't it ironic that the word *present* is the word we use for gift?)

HOW TO MAKE A PICKLE

Not only do I need to slow down to grow in my spiritual life, I also need to realize that spiritual growth is a slow process. Making pickles is an apt analogy to the way we grow as disciples. To make a pickle we first need to get a cucumber. Then we need to create the brine and vinegar solution for soaking the cucumber. If we dip the cucumber in the solution and quickly pull it out, all we will have is a baptized cucumber. In order for it to become a pickle, it needs to soak in the brine for six weeks or so. Slowly and imperceptibly, the solution works its way into the cucumber, changing it to a pickle.

Making pickles takes six weeks, but making an apprentice of Jesus takes much longer. The great preacher Graham Scroggie wrote, "Spiritual renewal is a gradual process. All growth is progressive, and the finer the organism, the longer the process." Human beings are finer organisms than cucumbers; there are many factors involved in our transformation. My mind, emotions and body are multifaceted. The human soul is a massive entity that changes very slowly.

I love the old story told by A. H. Strong:

> A student asked the President of his school whether he could not take a shorter course than the one prescribed. "Oh yes," replied the President, "but then it depends on what you want to be. When God wants to make an oak, He takes a hundred years, but when He wants to make a squash, He takes six months."

Strong goes on to explain that spiritual growth, in addition to being slow, is not *uniform*. Some years we may experience tremendous growth, and some we see very little change. An oak tree has only a couple of months of actual growth each year in terms of measurable expansion, says Strong. The rest of the year, the other ten months, are spent solidifying that growth.

THE TEN-THOUSAND-HOUR RULE

In *Outliers* Malcolm Gladwell shares his discoveries about exceptional people—those who lie outside the norm. Though it seems some people are born with exceptional talent, Gladwell's research led him to conclude:

> The emerging picture from studies is that ten thousand hours of practice is required to achieve the level of mastery associated with being a world-class expert in anything. . . . In study after study of composers, basketball players, chess players, master criminals and what have you, this number comes up again and again. . . . It seems that it takes the brain this long to assimilate all that it needs to know and achieve true mastery.

He cites Mozart as an example. Most people know that Mozart was composing music at the age of six. But Gladwell points out that he was not composing *good* music at six. His first good work was produced at age twenty-one, after fifteen years of hard work, and his best work was not written until his late twenties. Music critic Harold Schonberg actually said that, in this sense, Mozart "developed late"!

To become proficient at something takes a lot of time. But if someone wants to be exceptional, they need to put in ten thousand hours of practice. Please don't be discouraged by this! I share it only to put the process of transformation into proper perspective. Many Christians hope that within a few months of starting a Bible study or beginning a new prayer practice, they will see dramatic change. When they see little change, they usually feel they did something wrong or didn't try hard enough and discouragement sets in.

The truth is this: whatever we do to change, even the smallest steps, have an effect on us. Reading this book carefully and working to replace false narratives with the narratives of Jesus will help us make significant steps toward change. I am certain that the Holy Spirit comes alongside us and renovates our soul when we earnestly engage in the spiritual training exercises. But we must not expect massive changes overnight.

For example, I have been working on these narratives and engaging in these practices for over twenty-five years, and yet I remain a work in progress. But every month of every year I have seen positive growth in my life with God. Be encouraged. Change is slow, but it does take place. For many of you the change is already beginning. God is doing a good work in you, and you know it. Be confident that this is the beginning of new life in Christ. You must not have confidence in this or any other book, but in the good and beautiful God who is at work in you and has a plan for your life: "I am confident of this, that the one who began a good work among you will bring it to completion by the day of Jesus Christ" (Philippians 1:6).

ONLY THE BEGINNING

This book was written to help you fall in love with the God Jesus knows. We cannot enter into a deeper life with God unless we know and love him. This chapter is a hinge between this book and a second volume, *The Good and Beautiful Life*, which follows the same pattern as this one: replacing false narratives and engaging in spiritual disciplines that help embed new narratives in our souls. This second volume deals with areas of human failure, such as anger, lying, lust and worry. What Jesus says about these things is opposed to the narratives we hear from the world.

Once we have begun to "pickle" in Jesus' narratives about God, we can examine our own hearts and lives. Now that we have come to know the good and beautiful God, we are invited to the good and beautiful life. In the meantime, we must slow down and allow the narratives of Jesus to settle into our heart, mind and soul.

slowing Down

Slowing down is the way our soul works. Robert Barron says, "The deepest part of the soul likes to *go slow*, since it seeks to savor rather than to accomplish; it wants to rest in and contemplate the good rather than hurry off to another place." This is your assignment: slow down, savor, rest and contemplate. Slowing down the pace of our lives means eliminating hurry and limiting the demands and activities in our lives. Then we are more likely to take delight in our lives and make room for God.

In ages past, Christians engaged in ascetic practices (lengthy fasts and self-flagellation) to discipline themselves in order to grow closer to God. We need something altogether different in our modern culture. Paul Evdokimov aptly writes:

> Today the combat is not the same. We no longer need added pain. Hair shirts, chains and flagellation would risk uselessly breaking us. Today mortification would be liberation from every kind of addiction—speed, noise, alcohol, and all kinds of stimulants. *Asceticism would be necessary rest*, the discipline of regular periods of calm and silence, when one could regain the ability to stop for prayer and contemplation, even in the heart of all of the noise of the world.

I think he's right about our current way of life. We are driven by speed and stimulants, and thus the most needed discipline for us is to slow down, to calm down, and to make time for rest and contemplation.

MARGIN AND SLOWING

We cannot slow down until we know how to practice margin. (This is why margin was discussed in this book before slowing down.) We have to begin cutting out activities before we can change the pace of our lives. Matt Johnson, a coworker in The Apprentice Series material, is a living example of margin and slowing down. A successful assistant pastor for several years, Matt took on more responsibilities each year—largely because he's good at many things. At a certain point he realized that his busyness was affecting his spiritual life. After consulting with his wife, Matt asked the senior pastor if he could cut back on his work. This obviously meant a reduction in his salary, which Matt himself suggested.

Now on Mondays and Fridays Matt has extended times sitting at the feet of Jesus. As a friend I can tell you that the Christ who dwells in Matt is a great blessing to me and many others. To be sure, he "accomplishes" less, and he makes a little less money, but his soul has grown tremendously. Which is more important? Matt would be the first to tell you that what he has gained far outweighs what he has sacrificed. Matt lives at the right pace, is present where he is and brings Christ into every aspect of his life.

HOW TO PRACTICE SLOWING DOWN

- Think about the activities of the upcoming day. Instead of waiting until the last minute to go to your next activity, try leaving ten minutes early. Walk more slowly. Drive more slowly. When you arrive at your destination a bit earlier than usual, use the extra time to notice people and things around you. Breathe.

- Intentionally get in the slowest lane while driving, and the longest checkout line when shopping. Good luck with this one!

- Plan a meal with a friend or group of friends. Cook slowly. Enjoy the act and smells of cooking. Linger over your meal, spending an hour or two eating slowly, conversing and enjoying the blessing of food.

- Set aside an hour today to be a sloth (animals that move very slowly, sometimes taking ten minutes to climb a few feet). Move slowly. Take up to five minutes just to walk from the living room to the kitchen. Take a step and stop. Notice things. Breathe deeply. Be present to the present moment. Do everything at a deliberately slower speed.

Would I be in a coma? Dust, Dirty Dishes, Laundry

- Make a whole day a "slow day." Get up a little earlier so you can have time to linger over breakfast. If you are at work, do your work with a slower, more rhythmic pace (assuming your profession allows this; if you need to act quickly, do so without "hurrying"). Cut out TV and all forms of media for the day. Take time to watch a sunset, take a leisurely walk, watch kids play in the park. Sometime later in the evening, sketch out your thoughts about what living a slowed-down life would look like.

When you change speeds your internal system (your soul) will be thrown off of its usual pace and feelings of frustration will develop.

> "It seems that most believers have difficulty in realizing and facing up to the inexorable fact that God does not hurry in His development of our Christian life. He is working from and for eternity!"
>
> Miles J. Stanford

For example, when you force yourself to drive in the slow lane, you'll begin to feel your stomach churn a bit, and maybe you'll grind your teeth. Your body will be saying, "C'mon, hurry up, step on it, let's go," as it has been trained to do. You will need to die to that inward need. Don't worry—you can do this. It has not killed anyone so far.

FOR REFLECTION

Whether you are going through this material alone or with others, the following questions might be helpful as you reflect on your experience. Either way, it might be a good idea to answer these questions in your journal. If you are meeting with a group, bring your journal with you to help you remember your insights as you share your experiences.

1. Were you able to practice any of the exercises this week? If so, describe what you did and how you felt about it.

2. What, if anything, did you learn about God or yourself through the exercises?

3. Slowing down is countercultural. Describe the challenges you encountered. Will you keep trying to slow down in the future?

appendix

small group discussion guide

matthew johnson with christopher jason fox

In the fall of 2006 we were invited to participate in an experimental class being led by James Bryan Smith, which he called the Apprentice class. We knew Dr. Smith—his skill as a teacher, his grasp of spiritual formation—but none of us were prepared for the impact this class would have on our lives and ministries. It was amazing. It wasn't long before we were looking for ways to take this same teaching into the churches where we serve, and the results were no less profound. Along the way we have seen the truth of what Jim Smith says in the first chapter about community as one of the key components of transformation. This truth has been lived out by those of us who have worked through this book in small groups—reading, practicing and then discussing what we experienced. The result has been a deep healing of narratives, the joy of connecting on a personal level with others, and a life transformed to be more like that of Jesus. Out of these experiences, this discussion guide was created to help any-one gather a group of friends, family, a youth group, a small group, a Sunday school class or a book club together.

A group can range in size from two to twelve people. We have found that the ideal size for a group is five or six people. With a group of this size, you can simply read through the questions in the guide and share your thoughts and answers. Some groups find that they function well with shared leadership, perhaps rotating the point person from week to week. If the group has twelve or more members, it will work best to have a consistent appointed leader.

Each session is split into multiple segments. Use these segments in whatever way is most comfortable for your setting. Feel free to skip over questions or segments, as well as add questions of your own. In addition, you may want to spend time as a group looking at the questions sprinkled throughout each chapter, discussing anything you found particularly helpful or challenging.

Depending on the size of your group, following these discussion guides could take anywhere from sixty to ninety minutes. We have included estimates on how long each segment will take. If your group has more than six participants, expect the group time to last ninety minutes.

If you are the designated leader of a small group that is working through this book, you can either use this guide as a starting point, making your own creative changes as you prepare, or you can visit www.apprenticeofjesus.org to explore supplemental materials that give more options for class and discussion experiences. Through this site leaders can interact with each other and find additional resources.

May this simple guide serve as a tool in the hands of the Spirit to lead you to a deeper love of the good and beautiful God.

Matthew Johnson
with Christopher Jason Fox

Chapter 1: WHAT ARE YOU SEEKING?

OPENING TO GOD [5 MINUTES]

Begin with five minutes of silence followed by a brief prayer inviting God to guide the conversation. *Why 5 minutes of silence?* We live in a world that is filled with noise and distractions. It is easy to enter one conversation still processing the last conversation. In the midst of all this busyness it is also difficult to hear the whispering voice of God. When we gather with friends to share our spiritual journey, what we want is to hear God's voice in the lives of those around us. With a little silence we will be prepared to listen, so one option is to begin each gathering with some silence.

SOUL TRAINING [10-15 MINUTES]

If you are in a group of seven or more people, divide into small groups of three or four. Spend ten minutes discussing what you learned from the soul-training experience of sleep. To help everyone get started, share your thoughts on these questions.

1. Were you able to practice the discipline of sleep this week? If so, describe what you did and how you felt about it.

2. What, if anything, did you learn about God or yourself through the exercise?

ENGAGING THE CHAPTER [30-45 MINUTES]

The primary idea of this chapter is that most people want to change, but fail—not because they're not *trying,* but because they're not *training* properly.

[*Note:* Each week read through the questions before you begin discussion. Note any questions you especially want to discuss. Depending on your group size and the conversation, you may not have time to discuss all these questions.]

1. Have you ever tried to change something about yourself? What

process did you use? How successful were you in changing?

2. The author gives us a diagram for transformation (p. 24). It is made up of personal narratives, soul-training exercises, community and the Holy Spirit. Have any of these been a part of how you have changed in the past? Explain.

3. Our narratives are stories that shape the way we live. To help you understand the concept of narratives better, think of a story from your life that defines success for you. Talk about that with the group.

4. Many people are tempted (and have been taught) to practice spiritual disciplines to please God, when in fact they are a means of transforming the soul. How does that alter your approach to the practices you already do?

5. When has a small group of people spurred you on and encouraged you on your journey?

6. From the section on the work of the Holy Spirit (pp. 28-31), what insights did you gain about the Holy Spirit and how he impacts our narratives, soul training or sense of community?

ENGAGING THE WORD [10-15 MINUTES]
[*Note:* Take the time to have someone read the Scripture text aloud each week. It's good to hear it read even if it's also in front of you in a written format.]
Read John 1:38-39 aloud.

1. Listen to Jesus' words; imagine you are the disciple asking the question. What are you looking for?

2. When Jesus tells you to "come and see," what emotion do you feel?

GO IN PEACE [5 MINUTES]
Conclude by having one person in your group read these words from the first chapter aloud.

When the Spirit has changed our narratives sufficiently, we begin to think differently. As a result we begin to believe in and trust a good and loving God who is strong and powerful. We begin to see how Jesus lived a perfect life that we cannot live and offered that life to the Father on our behalf, setting us free from having to earn God's love and favor. And as we engage in soul-training exercises—especially in the context of community—our confidence that God is at work in and among us increases. This creates an inward change that manifests itself in outward behavior.

Now, when faced with an airport delay, we can take a deep breath and remember who we are. . . . We can endure these trials with love, joy, peace, patience and kindness. (p. 31)

Go from this place, savoring the good news that God is at work in and among you. Amen.

NEXT WEEK
In the next chapter we'll explore God's goodness. The soul-training practice for the week will be five minutes of daily silence and paying attention to the created world.

Chapter 2: GOD IS GOOD

OPENING TO GOD [5 MINUTES]
Begin with five minutes of silence followed by a brief prayer.

SOUL TRAINING [10-15 MINUTES]
Divide into small groups of three or four and spend time discussing what you learned from the two soul-training experiences. To help you begin, you might use these three questions:

1. What, if anything, did you learn about God or yourself through the exercises?

2. Was it hard for you to find five minutes for silence each day?

3. What stood out for you as you paid closer attention to the created world around you?

ENGAGING THE CHAPTER [20-30 MINUTES]

The primary focus of this chapter is wrestling with the commonly held narrative that God is an angry God, who punishes us for our sins, but the God Jesus knows and reveals is good—meaning there is nothing bad about God.

1. The author shares a story of being confronted by a friend who says that either his sin or his wife's sin had caused his daughter Madeline's illness. What was your reaction to that story?

2. Have you ever had times when you felt that God was punishing you for a sin, or perhaps had a friend tell you that was happening to you? If so, talk about that experience.

3. The author points out that many live by the narrative that says: "God is an angry judge. If you sin you will be punished." Has this narrative ever affected you? If so, where did that narrative come from?

4. Look back at the section called "The Good Only the Good Know" (pp. 46-47). St. Augustine had a brilliant insight when he shifted the discussion away from the "cause and effect" notion of sin and suffering, and taught instead about the "peculiar good" belonging to those who do good, and the evil that results from evil. For example, a person who goes about doing good will experience blessings unknown to those who do evil, such as inner contentment, the good feeling of having helped another, trust and so on. If time allows, tell stories of people you have known who have received the "good" because of their goodness.

ENGAGING THE WORD [15-30 MINUTES]
Read John 9 aloud.

1. As an onlooker, what do you see, hear and feel?

2. Watching Jesus in action in John 9, what do you learn about him?

3. What do you learn about human nature through the Pharisees, the disciples and the man who was born blind?

4. Are there any areas of your life where you feel God has punished you? If so, imagine yourself in the place of the man born blind. Allow yourself to hear Jesus' words, as if they are spoken to you.

GO IN PEACE [5-10 MINUTES]
Have a volunteer from the group read the quote below from the chapter. Then sit in silence and soak in these words to close your time together.

> Jesus said his Father was good. Jesus also refused to affirm the idea that external rewards and punishments are given by God on the basis of our good or bad works. Rain falls on the good and the bad. Sometimes we pray for rain (for our crops), and sometimes we pray that it will not rain (for our picnics). Both good and bad people get rained on, whether they want it or not. Jesus faced suffering, rejection and alienation, and the people jeered at him as he hung on the cross, questioning whether God was really with him. And Jesus believed. And he believes for me. (p. 49)

If you're comfortable doing so, offer prayers of praise and thanksgiving for the God who is good.

NEXT WEEK
In the next chapter we'll explore God's trustworthiness. The soul-training practice for the week will be counting your blessings.

Chapter 3: GOD IS TRUSTWORTHY

[*Note:* In this week's session the soul-training segment takes place following the chapter discussion.]

OPENING TO GOD [5 MINUTES]

Begin with five minutes of silence followed by a brief prayer.

ENGAGING THE CHAPTER [25-45 MINUTES]

The primary focus of this chapter is that we can trust God because Jesus trusted God—even as he entered into his suffering.

1. Have you ever done a team-building exercise? If so, describe your experience to the group. Did the exercise build trust? If so, what did it feel like to "trust your team"?

2. The author believes God is trustworthy because the God Jesus reveals would never do anything to harm us. God has no malice or evil intentions. How does this compare to your own definition of trustworthiness?

3. In the Lord's Prayer we encounter a God who is present, pure, powerful, who provides, pardons and protects (pp. 60-61). Which of these aspects of God is most comforting for you? Which one is the most difficult to grasp?

4. If you are in a group of six or more, divide into groups of three or four to discuss the following questions. [Allow about 10-15 minutes for this conversation and prayer.]

A "cup" (see pp. 64-65) is that aspect of our life that makes it difficult for us to trust God.

- Can you name a "cup" from your own life? What have you learned about God or yourself through that experience?

- The author tells us, "Jesus trusted his Abba, and I will also trust in the God I know to be good." How does it feel to know that you don't have to "force" yourself to say "all is well"?

- Whether you are in the midst of tragedy or not, it is amazing to see our story joined with God's story (pp. 65-67). How does this good news change your perspective and the way you spend your time and energy?

- If you're comfortable, spend time in prayer for one another, inviting God to join his story with yours.

SOUL TRAINING [10-15 MINUTES]

Near the end of the chapter the focus turns to the blessings we have received. If the group is large enough, divide into *new* groups of three to four and discuss what you learned from the soul-training practice of counting your blessings. It isn't necessary to share your list. Use these questions to help you begin:

1. What, if anything, did you learn about God or yourself through the exercise?

2. What were some of the things that made your list that surprised you? Why?

3. What similarities do you notice between everyone's lists?

ENGAGING THE WORD [10-15 MINUTES]

Read Matthew 26:36-44 aloud.

1. Picture the events in this text. What emotions does this scene stir within you?

2. How does this moment from Jesus' life impact your ability to trust God?

GO IN PEACE [5 MINUTES]

Have two or three volunteers read the list of six descriptors of God (God is present, God is pure, God is powerful, God provides, God pardons and God protects) slowly, once each, then have a few minutes of silence.

End the silence with these words: Go in the assurance of a God who can be trusted.

NEXT WEEK

In the next chapter we'll explore God's generosity. The soul-training practice for the week will be living and breathing Psalm 23—enjoy!

Chapter 4: GOD IS GENEROUS

OPENING TO GOD [5 MINUTES]

Have someone in the group read through the list of characteristics of God from chapter three (God is present, God is pure, God is powerful, God provides, God pardons and God protects), and then allow five minutes for silence. Conclude the silence with a brief prayer.

SOUL TRAINING [10-15 MINUTES]

In groups of three or four discuss the soul-shaping practice of living and breathing Psalm 23. Use these reflection questions to help your conversation:

1. Were you able to practice the exercise this week? If so, describe what you did and how you felt about it.

2. What, if anything, did you learn about God or yourself through the exercise?

3. What was the most meaningful verse or phrase of Psalm 23 for you?

ENGAGING THE CHAPTER [25-45 MINUTES]

The primary focus of this chapter is that we do not earn God's love, favor, forgiveness or acceptance. God is generous and gives them to us freely.

1. The false narrative explored in this chapter is, "Love and forgiveness are commodities that are exchanged for performance. God's love, acceptance and forgiveness must be merited by right living.

What God most wants is for us not to sin and instead to do good"
(p. 77). What effect does this narrative have on your relationship
with God?

2. The author points out, "To say that sin has consequences is different than saying that because of our sin God entirely rejects
us" (p. 78). How would you put into your own words this idea
that sin has consequences, but our sin does *not* lead God to
reject us?

3. The overarching story of the Bible reveals a God of grace. Certain
minor narratives may seem to contradict this major narrative, but
the minor narratives must be interpreted only in terms of undeserved and unearned love (see p. 79). How does this way of reading Scripture resonate with you? In what ways does it help your
reading of the Bible? In what ways does it make you
uncomfortable?

4. We are assured that God's love is not earned, and that what God
wants from us is simply for us to know his love, which will naturally lead us to love in return. If it's true that God's love is not
earned, what would you do differently tomorrow? Why?

5. A. W. Tozer writes, "What comes into our mind when we think
about God is the most important thing about us" (p. 88). If you are
in a group of six or more, split into groups of three or four. Describe to your small group the first thing that comes into your
mind when you think about God. In what ways does this thought
shape your daily life?

ENGAGING THE WORD [15-20 MINUTES]
Read Matthew 20:1-15 aloud.

1. If this was the only story you knew about God what would you
conclude?

2. Silently consider how you have experienced God's generosity. As

events and blessings come to mind, do you notice anything that changes inside of you?

GO IN PEACE [5 MINUTES]

Have a volunteer from your group read the following story out loud. Try to imagine this scene as the story is read:

> One morning this past spring I noticed a young couple with an infant at an airport departure gate. The baby was staring intently at other people, and as soon as he recognized a human face, no matter whose it was, no matter if it was young or old, pretty or ugly, bored or happy or worried-looking he would respond with absolute delight. It was beautiful to see. Our drab departure gate had become the gate of heaven. And as I watched that baby play with any adult who would allow it, I felt as awe-struck as Jacob, because I realized that this is how God looks at us, staring into our faces in order to be delighted, to see the creature he made and called good, along with the rest of creation. . . . I suspect that only God, and well-loved infants, can see this way. (p. 87).

Go in peace, and live gladly in the knowledge of God's generosity toward you.

NEXT WEEK

In the next chapter we'll explore God's radical love. The soul-training practice for the week will be *lectio divina*, which is explained at the end of the chapter. You may want to practice *lectio divina* several times during the coming week.

Chapter 5: GOD IS LOVE

OPENING TO GOD [5 MINUTES]

Begin with five minutes of silence. At the conclusion of the five minutes, offer a brief prayer.

SOUL TRAINING [10-15 MINUTES]

Divide into small groups of three or four and discuss what you learned from the soul-training practice of *lectio divina*. Use these reflection questions to help your conversation.

1. Were you able to do the *lectio divina* exercise? If so, describe what you did and how you felt about it.

2. What, if anything, did you learn about God or yourself through the exercise?

ENGAGING THE CHAPTER [25-45 MINUTES]

The primary focus of this chapter is that most people believe that love is conditional, that it's based on one's behavior. Thus, most people believe that God loves us only when we're good. Jesus told of a God who loves without condition—a God who even loves sinners.

1. The false narrative explored in this chapter is that God only loves us when we're good. The author gives us the image of a God sitting on a swivel chair, turning toward us when we're "good," and turning away when we're "bad" (p. 94). What image would you use to describe God's reaction to your sin?

2. By looking at various Scripture passages, this chapter unpacks the reality that God loves sinners. How does it make you feel to know that God loves you—just as you are?

3. John 3:16 tells us that God loves the world, meaning that God loves everyone—including our enemies, those who have wounded us and those who just irritate us. How does it make you feel to know that God loves people you don't love? You might silently consider naming those you struggle to love (including yourself).

If you're in a group of six or more, split into groups of three or four to share your thoughts on questions four and five below. If necessary, review "The Prodigal Father" (pp. 99-101) and "The Elder Brother and Me" (pp. 101-2).

4. From the parable of the prodigal son, which of the sons can you relate to more? Can you relate to the father? If so, in what way(s)?

5. The author writes, "Our self-righteousness does not turn God from us, but us from God. It is not my sin that moves me away from God, it is my refusal of grace, both for myself and for others" (p. 102). What is your reaction to this statement? In what ways does your own self-righteousness hold you back from God? How can we recognize self-righteousness in our lives?

6. If you have split into groups of three or four, regroup and have someone in the group slowly read aloud the poem "Love (III)" (pp. 103-4), allowing everyone else to picture the encounter with Love.

ENGAGING THE WORD [15-20 MINUTES]

Lectio divina can be done as a group. Use the Scripture printed below as your text (Matthew 9:12-13). Before you start, decide who will read the Scripture each time.

- The first time the Scripture is read, let the Word soak into your mind. Allow a few minutes of silence.

- The second time the Scripture is read, note any word that God seems to be emphasizing. After the second reading, anyone in the group can share the word or phrase that spoke to them, but they should not elaborate.

- Read the passage a third time. This time allow God to reveal to you the significance of this word. Spend three to five minutes in silence, conversing with God. After the silence, anyone who is willing can share what they felt God spoke to them through the passage.

Those who are well have no need of a physician, but those who are sick. Go and learn what this means, "I desire mercy, not sacrifice." For I have come to call not the righteous but sinners. (Matthew 9:12-13)

GO IN PEACE
Go in peace, and live gladly in the knowledge of God's love for you.

NEXT WEEK
In the next chapter we'll study God's holiness. The soul-shaping practice is margin, which will be explained in depth at the end of the chapter. Margin is something you'll want a full week to practice before you gather again to discuss, so plan on reading the chapter and soul-training section early.

Chapter 6: GOD IS HOLY

OPENING TO GOD [5 MINUTES]
Begin with five minutes of silence. At the conclusion of the five minutes, offer a brief prayer.

SOUL TRAINING [10-15 MINUTES]
Divide into small groups of three or four and discuss what you learned from the soul-training practice of margin. Use these reflection questions to start your conversation:

1. Were you able to develop margin in any way this week? If so, describe what you did and how you felt about it.

2. As you tried to develop margin in your life, what was most difficult? What was most rewarding?

3. How do you plan to practice the discipline of margin in the future?

4. What, if anything, did you learn about God or yourself through the exercise?

ENGAGING THE CHAPTER [25-35 MINUTES]
The primary focus of this chapter is that God is love and God is also holy. God's wrath toward sin is an action that reflects that love and holiness.

1. Chapter six addresses two false narratives. The first is that God is always angry and wrathful toward us. The second false narrative is that God doesn't care about sin at all and is more of a "teddy bear." Which of these two narratives do you identify with more? Why?

2. To love is "to will the good of another," according to Dallas Willard (p. 119). When this understanding of love comes in contact with our sin, the result is God's wrath, because "God is fiercely and forcefully opposed to the things that destroy his precious people" (p. 121). What would you say to a friend who wanted to understand how a loving God could be wrathful?

3. On pages 121-22 the author gives the example of MADD as a rare instance when human wrath could be compared to God's wrath. Can you think of any other human examples?

4. We are given this wonderful quote from George MacDonald: "love loves unto purity" (p. 123). What thoughts and feelings do you have when you consider that God longs to remove everything from your life that would destroy you?

5. "God will not violate the choices we make. People may choose to bar God from their life. Thus the doors of hell are locked from the inside" (p. 125). How is this vision of hell similar to or different from your own understanding?

6. The chapter concludes with the important point that we must first trust in God's love and forgiveness before we can begin to understand God's holiness. The first five chapters of this book unpack God's love and goodness. What impact have the previous five chapters had in preparing you to understand God's holiness?

ENGAGING THE WORD [15-20 MINUTES]
Read Hebrews 12:18-29 aloud.

1. This passage begins by contrasting the covenant made on Mount

Sinai with the covenant made by Jesus' blood. What images of God's holiness do you see throughout the passage?

2. One way of interpreting this passage is to view pieces in our lives that can be "shaken" and removed as those pieces that are opposed to God. On the other hand, the kingdom we are receiving is the unshakable kingdom of God—the "with-God life." Has there ever been a time in your life when you felt shaken and eventually purified? Did you see God's hand at work through that situation, and if so, in what way?

3. How does it feel to know that while purification can be painful, it ultimately leads to deeper intimacy with God?

GO IN PEACE [5 MINUTES]

Have a volunteer from the group read the quote below from the chapter. Then sit in silence and soak in these words to close your time together.

> God is against my sin because he is for me. And if I am for sin, God stands against those desires, MacDonald is saying, because they cause my destruction. I would not have it any other way. To be sure, I am prone to excusing my sin or rationalizing my weaknesses, but God is not in that business. Though we are now reconciled through Christ, God is not indifferent to my sin. It hurts me, and therefore it hurts God—because God loves me.
>
> God does not make me feel bad or shame me into better behavior. Nor does he use fear or guilt. God's method of change is the highest of all. God's holy love burns the dross of sin out of our lives. It is God's kindness that leads to genuine repentance (Romans 2:4). As MacDonald said, "love loves unto purity." (pp. 123-24)

God's love is loving you "unto purity." Go in the assurance of God's deep desire for your good.

NEXT WEEK

In the next chapter we'll explore God's self-sacrificial nature. The soul-training practice for the week will be reading the entire Gospel of John. You'll need to allow ample time for this exercise (one to three hours). Some groups have done their reading together out loud; you may wish to consider this option as well.

Chapter 7: GOD IS SELF-SACRIFICING

OPENING TO GOD [5 MINUTES]

Begin with five minutes of silence. At the conclusion of the five minutes, offer a brief prayer.

SOUL TRAINING [10-15 MINUTES]

Divide into small groups of three or four and discuss your experience of reading the Gospel of John. To help you begin, you might use these questions:

1. What did you notice that you hadn't noticed before in previous readings of the Gospel of John?

2. How would you describe the effect this week's reading had on you?

3. If time allows, spend a few minutes looking over past soul-training exercises. What exercises are you still doing? What impact are they continuing to have on your life?

ENGAGING THE CHAPTER [25-35 MINUTES]

The primary focus of this chapter is that self-sacrifice is an essential part of the character of God.

1. This chapter begins with a story of the author's sister being uncertain of the necessity of the cross. Before reading this chapter, how would you have explained Jesus' need to die on the cross?

2. On pages 135-38 the author gives us an imaginary conversation

with Athanasius, based on the book *On the Incarnation*. Look back over this section and share parts that you really enjoyed and parts that raised questions for you.

3. The author introduces the idea that God feels both joy and pain. How do you feel about a God who feels pain? Why?

4. "Maybe vulnerability is true strength" (p. 140). This idea runs against cultural narratives that many of us hold. Who in your own life have you seen demonstrate strength through vulnerability?

5. "At the heart of the universe is this one principle: *self-sacrifice is the highest act*. The grain of wheat must die in order to give life. The cosmos reflects the nature of the God who created it" (p. 141). Can you name other examples of creation revealing this principle? Have you ever considered it a characteristic of God to be self-sacrificing? What impact does this statement have on your own feelings toward God?

6. What was your reaction to the Brennan Manning story (pp. 142-43), specifically the understanding that Jesus could not have done any more for us?

ENGAGING THE WORD [15-25 MINUTES]

The following Scripture study follows a *lectio divina* format. Use the Scripture on the next page as your text (Philippians 2:6-11). Before you begin, decide who will read the Scripture each time.

• The first time the Scripture is read, allow the Word to soak into your mind. Allow a few minutes of silence.

• The second time the Scripture is read, note any word that God seems to be emphasizing. After the second reading, anyone in the group can share the word or phrase that spoke to them, but they should not elaborate.

• Read the passage a third time. This time allow God to reveal to you the significance of this word. Spend three to five minutes in silence, conversing with God. After the silence, anyone who is willing can share what they felt God spoke to them through the passage.

[Jesus], though he was in the form of God,
    did not regard equality with God
    as something to be exploited,
but emptied himself,
    taking the form of a slave,
    being born in human likeness.
And being found in human form,
    he humbled himself
    and became obedient to the point of death—
    even death on a cross.

Therefore God also highly exalted him
    and gave him the name
    that is above every name,
so that at the name of Jesus
    every knee should bend,
    in heaven and on earth and under the earth,
and every tongue should confess
    that Jesus Christ is Lord,
    to the glory of God the Father. (Philippians 2:6-11)

GO IN PEACE [5 MINUTES]

Have a volunteer from the group read the quote below. Then sit in silence for a few minutes soaking in these words to close your time together.

Here is a key principle of the kingdom of God: What we let go of will never be lost but becomes a thing of beauty. No wonder the manger and the cross are two of the most beautiful images this world has ever seen. In the incarnation God, who created millions of spinning galaxies, chose to become vulnerable, and in so doing, heaven came down and kissed the earth. In the crucifixion God, who could not die, subjected himself to death, and in so doing lifted the whole world to himself. (p. 145)

God loves you so much he became vulnerable for you. Go with that amazing good news.

NEXT WEEK

In the next chapter we'll explore how God transforms us. The soul-training practice for the week is solitude. You'll need to schedule time for this practice and let others in your life who may be affected by it know when you'll be doing it.

Chapter 8: GOD TRANSFORMS

OPENING TO GOD [5 MINUTES]

Begin with five minutes of silence. At the conclusion of the five minutes, offer a brief prayer.

SOUL TRAINING [10-15 MINUTES]

Divide into small groups of three or four and spend ten to fifteen minutes discussing your experience of solitude. Use these reflection questions to get your conversation started:

1. Begin by sharing how your time of solitude went. Remember that for some people this discipline can be very difficult and even frustrating, while for others this exercise is very energizing.

2. One of the aims of the time of solitude is to give you the ability to "take off your masks" and simply be who you truly are in the presence of God. This is a powerful and complex idea, so it may be helpful to refer to page 167. Would that describe your experience with this exercise? Explain.

3. What, if anything, did you learn about God or yourself through the exercise?

ENGAGING THE CHAPTER [25-45 MINUTES]

The primary focus of this chapter is that the resurrection of Jesus transforms us into new beings (in whom Christ dwells), which empowers and guides how we live as Christians.

1. The author opens the chapter with a story about a friend of his named Carey, who did not want to sin, and yet continued to sin. Can you relate to Carey's struggle to overcome sin? What have you done in the past to address areas of sin in your life? How effective were those efforts?

2. Read this out loud: "In Christ I am no longer to be defined by sin. I have been reconciled. Sin has been defeated" (p. 153). What is the implication of this statement in your daily life?

3. "Christians are people Christ dwells in" (p. 154). As a group, spend a few minutes in silence. During that time, imagine Jesus "dwelling" within you. After the silence, if you're comfortable, share what this reality means to you.

4. As ones "indwelt by Christ," we are not under the law; however, not everything is "beneficial" for us. Our choices no longer *define* who we are; instead, our choices are made *in light of* who we are. Reflect on the last twenty-four hours of your life. Call to mind the choices that you made. What choices did you make to "determine who you are"? What choices did you make "in light of who you are"? How would your day have been different if you had made more decisions in light of who you are?

5. The author gives us this amazing paradox: "We minister out of our brokenness. We heal others through our vulnerability because that is where Christ shines most brightly" (p. 163). In what ways are you broken? How might the light of Christ shine through those wounds?

ENGAGING THE WORD [15-20 MINUTES]
Read John 15:1-5 aloud.

1. The author gives us this definition for "abide": "To abide means to rest in and rely on Jesus, who is not outside of us, judging us, but is inside of us, empowering us. The more deeply we're aware of our identity in Christ and his presence and power with us, the more naturally we'll do this. We must get our narrative right and practice spiritual exercises to deepen our awareness of truth. In the end, Jesus' way is easy. He said that his yoke was easy and his burden was light (Matthew 11:30). Typically, we try to do what we think Jesus wants us to do . . . by [our] own strength. We can't do that. But we 'can do all things through Christ who strengthens' us (Philippians 4:13)" (p. 159). Write your own definition for what it means to "abide" in Christ, based on the author's definition. If you're comfortable, share your definition with the group.

2. Read John 15:4-5 again. What, if any, practices do you have in your life that help you "abide" in Christ?

GO IN PEACE [5 MINUTES]
End your time together by saying to each other in your group these words of good news: You were meant to house the fullness of God!

NEXT WEEK
The next chapter looks at the slow process of spiritual transformation. The soul-shaping practice for the week is slowing down.

Chapter 9: HOW TO MAKE A PICKLE

OPENING TO GOD [5 MINUTES]
Begin with five minutes of silence. At the conclusion of the five minutes, offer a brief prayer.

SOUL TRAINING [15-20 MINUTES]

Divide into groups of three or four to discuss your experience of slowing down. Use these reflection questions to help your conversation:

1. Slowing down is countercultural in our day. Describe the challenges you encountered. Will you keep trying to slow down in the future?

2. How would you describe the level of hurry in your life? What impact is the hurry in your life having on your relationship with God and others?

3. What, if anything, did you learn about God or yourself through the exercises?

ENGAGING THE CHAPTER [25-40 MINUTES]

The primary focus of this chapter is that to live an authentic and effective Christian life we must slow down the pace of our lives and become aware of the present moment.

1. The first part of the chapter (pp. 173-79) explores how our view of time evolved into "tyranny of the urgent" and even regarding humanity as a machine designed to produce tasks with efficiency. Discuss your experiences of being in the workplace, and the expectations placed on your performance.

2. The author reminds us that "we cannot love, think, eat, laugh or pray in a hurry" (p. 180). Looking back over the last week, what did you attempt to do in a hurry that can't be done in a hurry? When did you slow down and experience some of the blessings that come from slowing down?

3. "Too many of us are trying to serve God without listening to God. There will be time to serve, but listening to Jesus always takes precedence" (p. 181). Why do you think we're tempted to serve God without listening to God? What impact do your old narra-

tives about God have on your need to be busy with God-work?

4. The author gives us this illustration from A. H. Strong: "A student asked the President of his school whether he could not take a shorter course than the one prescribed. 'Oh yes,' replied the President, 'but then it depends on what you want to be. When God wants to make an oak, He takes a hundred years, but when He wants to make a squash, He takes six months.' Strong goes on to explain that spiritual growth, in addition to being slow, is also not *uniform*. Some years we may experience tremendous growth, and some we see very little change. An oak tree has only a couple of months of actual growth each year in terms of measurable expansion, says Strong. The rest of the year, the other ten months, are spent solidifying that growth" (p. 186). Reflecting on your spiritual journey over the last year, when have you experienced growth and when have you experienced solidifying? How about the last five and/or ten years?

5. Have someone from the group read this quote out loud to conclude your time of engaging the chapter:

Why is eliminating hurry from our lives so crucial? When we eliminate hurry we become present, or more specifically, present to the present moment in all of its glory. We become aware of our surroundings. We see colors and smell smells; we hear hushed sounds and can actually feel the wind in our faces. In short, we "show up" and experience the fullness of life. And that includes, not least of all, being present to God. If I am to live well as a Christian, I need to be constantly connected to God. Hurry is not part of a well-lived life. (p. 183)

ENGAGING THE WORD [15-20 MINUTES]
Read aloud Luke 10:38-42.

1. We are often tempted to view Martha and Mary as having two

personality types: Martha is the active busybody and Mary is the contemplative. But based on the author's insights we can see that the issue is not their personalities; it's the choices they made at that particular moment: Martha chose to serve, while Mary chose to listen. What are the ways that you regularly listen to Jesus? What activities tempt you away from those times of listening?

2. Name specific ways you as a group can support and encourage each other to continue listening to Jesus.

GO IN PEACE [15-20 MINUTES]
Spend fifteen to twenty minutes sharing with your group what you have gained by sharing this journey with them. Discuss this question: How has this group blessed you during these last several weeks?

LOOKING FORWARD [15 MINUTES]
Your study of *The Good and Beautiful God* has come to an end, but there are many options for your group. One option would be to begin the next book in The Apprentice Series, *The Good and Beautiful Life* (available January 2010). The two books are designed to go together. *The Good and Beautiful Life* explores the narratives of Jesus, and how those who have been "pickling" in his message are being set free from struggles with anger, lust, lying, self-righteousness and so on. The book takes a close look at the Sermon on the Mount.

Another option would be for members of the current group to form new groups and invite their friends to go through *The Good and Beautiful God* together. This second option is a great way to continue "pickling" in these narratives and falling more deeply in love with God. Whatever option you choose, select a date for your group to begin.

Notes

Chapter 1: What Are You Seeking?

p. 23 snap him water-soaked footballs: This story was told by Rick Reilly in his column, "Life of Reilly," in *Sports Illustrated,* February 12, 2007, p. 78.

p. 24 triangle of transformation: I have borrowed and modified the concept of a triangle of transformation from Dallas Willard. Dallas's triangle consists of The Spiritual Disciplines, Ordinary Events of Life and the Action of the Holy Spirit. My triangle is different, but contains some of the same elements.

p. 24 "the central function": Fredric Jameson, *The Political Unconscious: Narrative as a Socially Symbolic Act* (Ithaca, N.Y.: Cornell University Press, 1981), quoted in Alan Parry and Robert E. Doan, *Story Revisions: Narrative Therapy in the Postmodern World* (New York: Guilford Press, 1994), p. 24.

p. 25 "dream in narrative": Attributed to Barbara Hardy, quoted in Alasdair MacIntyre, *After Virtue: A Study in Moral-Theory* (Notre Dame, Ind.: University of Notre Dame Press, 1981), quoted in Parry and Doan, *Story Revisions,* p. 3.

p. 28 But the Holy Spirit is not often the focus of our lives: The exception being our charismatic and Pentecostal brothers and sisters who remind us of the role of the Spirit in our lives.

p. 29 our relationship with Jesus as Lord: See Tom Smail's book *The Giving Gift: The Holy Spirit in Person* (Eugene, Ore.: Wipf & Stock, 1994), p. 13.

p. 33 "we need rest more today": Arch Hart, quoted in Siang-Yang Tan, *Rest* (Ann Arbor, Mich.: Servant, 2000). All of the data in this paragraph and the next come from his chapter titled "Sleep," pp. 109-23.

p. 35 tips to help you fall asleep: These tips are a condensed and modified version of a set of suggestions in Dr. Tan's book in which he offers a list of ideas taken from Archibald Hart's book *The Anxiety Cure* (Nashville: Word, 1999), pp. 204-6.

Chapter 2: God Is Good

p. 41 "punishments of love": Raymond Brown, *The Gospel According to John I-XII,* vol. 1 (New York: Doubleday, 1966), note on John 9:2-3.

p. 41 God's 9/11 punishment: Jerry Falwell and Pat Robertson took this position within hours of the attacks. They were soon heavily criticized and later recanted.

p. 41   Study of conservative Christans: Funded by the Templeton Foundation, the Baylor Institute for Studies of Religion conducted a survey of Americans' religious beliefs and attitudes. Their findings began to be released in spring 2007.

p. 42   "you will all perish just as they did": Jesus' words do not refer to some impending physical harm or death that will come to people who do not shape up morally. "The death in view here is spiritual, not physical" (Earl D. Radmacher, ed., *Nelson's New Illustrated Bible Commentary* [Nashville: Thomas Nelson, 1999]), meaning something worse than death can happen to a person, namely, living without God.

p. 43   sin in the womb: New Testament scholar Merrill Tenney notes, "If a person suffered from any ailment, it must have been because his parents or grandparents had committed some sin against God. To this they added the thought that perhaps he might have sinned before birth, whether as an embryo or in a preexistent state. Such a concept appears in the rabbinical writings" (Merrill C. Tenney and Richard N. Longenecker, *John and Acts*, The Expositor's Bible Commentary, vol. 9 [Grand Rapids: Zondervan, 1981], p. 101).

p. 43   Blindness, it was believed: Adam Clarke states, "Most of the Asiatic nations believed in the doctrine of transmigration . . . and profess to tell precisely the sin which the person committed in another body, by the afflictions he endures in this." Another example, a person who suffers from headaches must have "spoken irreverently to father or mother" (Adam Clarke, *The New Testament of Our Lord and Saviour Jesus Christ*, vol. 1 [Nashville: Abingdon, 1911], p. 584).

p. 44   Tenney and Longenecker, *John and Acts*.

p. 45   "We do not know why": Augustine, quoted in James Walsh and P. G. Walsh, *Divine Providence & Human Suffering* (Wilmington, Del.: Michael Glazier, 1985), p. 95.

p. 46   "Rather we must seek out": Ibid.

p. 47   "When we come to Judgment Day": Augustine *City of God* 20.2, quoted in ibid.

p. 53   "become deeply absorbed in creation": Maureen Conroy, *Experiencing God's Tremendous Love: Entering into Relational Prayer* (Neptune, N.J.: Upper Room Spiritual Center, 1989), p. 23.

Chapter 3: God Is Trustworthy

p. 57   I invited him to tell his story: Those in the field of narrative therapy refer to this as "externalizing the story," wherein a person is able to look at the story as separate from him- or herself. In doing so the individual discovers that the story has an origin and a history, a life of its own. This is an essential step in deconstructing false narratives.

p. 57   Abba: *Abba* is an Aramaic word. Even though our New Testament is written in Greek, Aramaic was the common language of the Jewish people of

Jesus' day. That is why scholars believe when the Gospel writers tell us that Jesus addressed God as Abba, we are hearing the exact word he used. And because the Gospel writers intentionally used this Aramaic word even though they were writing in Greek, it is likely that Jesus used the word so much so that they could not exclude it.

p. 58   "Dear Father": Thomas Smail says that C. F. D. Moule and Joachim Jeremias, two leading New Testament scholars, "both agree that the best English translation of Abba is simply Dear Father" (*The Forgotten Father* [1980; reprint, Eugene, Ore.: Wipf & Stock, 2001], p. 39).

p. 58   "The intimate word": C. F. D. Moule, quoted in ibid.

p. 59   "proper fatherhood resides in God": Karl Barth, *Dogmatics in Outline* (London: SCM Press, 1949), p. 43, quoted in ibid., p. 58.

p. 60   In Jewish cosmology: In Jewish cosmology there are several layers of heaven, sometimes as few as three or as many as seven. The first level of heaven is the atmosphere around us. In Jesus' baptism, the stoning of Stephen (Acts 7) and Peter's vision (Acts 10), the "heavens" were opened, or, to be more accurate, the invisible heavenly realm around them became visible, even audible.

p. 61   "At the heart of God": Richard Foster, *Celebration of Discipline* (San Francisco: HarperSanFrancisco, 1978), p. 125.

p. 65   "The Father that Jesus addresses": Smail, *The Forgotten Father,* p. 37.

p. 66   "Our thoughts are not Your thoughts": The prayer came from a book called *For the Sick and the Suffering,* comp. Thomas Hopko, trans. David Anderson (Syosset, N.Y.: Orthodox Chuch in America, 1983). The actual prayer is called, "A Prayer for a Child in Great Suffering and Pain," (p. 31). Father Paul (who is now Right Reverend Paul Hodge) and I did not know we would be going to a hospital that day. The fact that he had this book with him was one of the many provisions of God we experienced that day.

p. 66   a metanarrative, which is the story: I use the term *metanarrative* in two senses. First, I use it to represent a larger narrative, which is the story God is writing. Second, the prefix *meta* means "change," and thus a metanarrative is also a narrative that leads to change.

p. 67   "A lecturer to a group of businessmen": George Buttrick, *Prayer* (New York: Abingdon-Cokesbury, 1942), quoted in Richard J. Foster and James Bryan Smith, *Devotional Classics* (San Francisco: HarperSanFrancisco, 1992), p. 101.

p. 70   If you are having trouble getting started: Jan Dargatz, *10,000 Things to Praise God For* (Nashville: Thomas Nelson, 1993).

p. 72   "When good is found": David Crowder, *The Praise Habit: Finding God in Sunshine and Sushi* (Colorado Springs: NavPress, 2004), pp. 13-14.

Chapter 4: God Is Generous

p. 75   "The process of spiritual formation": Dallas Willard, *Renovation of the Heart* (Colorado Springs: NavPress, 2002), pp. 101-2.

p. 79   the major narrative of the Bible is grace: I want to be very clear that I do not believe in "universalism," the belief that all people will be saved and go to heaven, and no one will be sent to hell. Universalism is not a biblical narrative but is a humanly constructed narrative. Jesus spoke about hell, and it was clearly a part of his narrative.

p. 80   God is good, you are bad, try harder: Henry Cloud said this in his talk "Action Steps for Monday" at the Leadership Summit at Willow Creek Community Church 2006.

p. 80   the struggle of some of the Jewish Christians: One Bible commentary notes that "the passage concerns true believers in Jesus, who are Jewish, and under persecution are tempted to mesh in with the Jewish religion and its rituals from which they had been freed in Christ" (Earl D. Radmacher, *Nelson's New Illustrated Bible Commentary* [Nashville: Thomas Nelson, 1999]).

p. 81   You are about to hear Jesus tell a story about God: Many Bible scholars believe that the quickest way to understand the teaching of Jesus is to study and reflect on the parables, which are succinct stories that reveal a great deal about God and his kingdom.

p. 82   eighteen thousand men out of work: This is according to Josephus *Antiquities of the Jews* 20:219.

p. 83   a similar parable was told by Jewish rabbis: Joachim Jeremias, *The Parables of Jesus* (Upper Saddle River, N.J.: Prentice Hall, 1954), pp. 138-39. Jeremias notes, however, that it is difficult to know if Jesus' parable was told before or after that of the other rabbis. If the rabbinical version precedes, then Jesus was taking a familiar story and adding a shocking ending, though Jeremias doubts this. Either way, the important thing to note is how different their interpretations are.

p. 83   "In the parable of Jesus": Ibid., p. 139.

p. 84   "Jesus reveals a God": Brennan Manning, talk given at Hilltop Urban Church, Wichita, Kansas.

p. 87   "One morning this past spring": Kathleen Norris, *Amazing Grace* (New York: Riverhead Books, 1998), p. 150, quoted in Peter Van Breeman, *The God Who Won't Let Go* (Notre Dame, Ind.: Ave Maria, 2001), p. 23.

p. 88   "What comes into our mind": A. W. Tozer, *The Knowledge of the Holy* (San Francisco: Harper & Row, 1961), p. 9.

p. 90   God even prepares a "table": The rule of hospitality was to guarantee the safety of a guest. If a person evaded his enemies, he was safe while dining in the tent with his hosts. It may be that the psalmist is imaging a situation where even one's enemies are invited to the banquet. I doubt that is a correct interpretation, but in light of Jesus' teaching about loving and blessing and praying for one's enemies, I like to imagine that everyone is included—even those who don't deserve to be.

Chapter 5: God Is Love

p. 97   when they catch him eating with sinners: The Pharisees are often depicted as "the bad guys" in the Gospels, but in truth, they, like all of us, were simply living out their narratives. They believed a narrative which said that only a strict adherence to the Mosaic law by God's people would bring the Messiah and restore Israel.

p. 98   "Here is the revelation bright as the evening star": Brennan Manning, *The Ragamuffin Gospel* (Sisters, Ore.: Multnomah Books, 1990), pp. 19-20.

p. 98   "For God so loved": I am crediting this famous verse to the actual words of Jesus and not to the Gospel writer John, though it is difficult to know exactly who is speaking. Many translations, including the New American Standard Bible, have John 3:12-16 in red letters because it seems likely that from John 3:10 to 3:21 Jesus is the speaker.

p. 99   parable of the father's love: This is the title New Testament scholar Joachim Jeremias suggests in his book *The Parables of Jesus* (Upper Saddle River, N.J.: Prentice-Hall, 1954), p. 128.

p. 100   a stunning and disrespectful request: The second son would be entitled to only one-third of the land, and in this parable he doesn't keep it as an investment but sells it. In so doing the entire family would suffer because the estate would be sold off. The father was not required to grant this request, and Jesus' hearers would have been shocked by this outrageous act of disrespect.

p. 100   He asks for his servants to bring: The robe signifies honor, the ring symbolizes authority, and the shoes indicate freedom (slaves did not wear shoes).

p. 101   Jesus' primary storytelling aim: Jeremias refers to this parable as an "apologetic parable" designed to respond to those who criticized him for comporting with sinners (*Parables of Jesus*, p. 132).

p. 106   "the judge judged in our place": A phrase made popular by Karl Barth in his *Church Dogmatics* 4.1.

p. 108   reading select passages of the Hebrew Bible: The selected passages were Deuteronomy 6:4-9, 11:13-21 and Numbers 15:37-41. This is explained in "Lectio Divina," in *The Upper Room Dictionary of Christian Spiritual Formation*, ed. Keith Beasley-Topliffe (Nashville: Upper Room Books, 2003), p. 167.

Chapter 6: God Is Holy

p. 116   "a God without wrath": H. Richard Niebuhr, *The Kingdom of God in America* (Middletown, Conn.: Wesleyan University Press, 1988), p. 193.

p. 119   "The concept of God's wrath": Albrecht Ritschl, *Die Christliche Lehre von der Rechtfertigung und Versöhnung (The Christian Doctrine on Justification and Reconciliation)*, vol. 2 (Bonn, 1889), p. 154.

p. 120   "the wrath of Yahweh": "Wrath of God," in *The Anchor Bible Dictionary*,

Gary A. Herion, Astrid B. Beck and David Noel Freedman, vol. 6 (New York: Doubleday, 1992), p. 989.

p. 121   "God's wrath must be understood": Ibid.

p. 121   "God's wrath in the Bible": J. I. Packer, *Knowing God* (Downers Grove., Ill: InterVarsity Press, 1973), p. 151.

p. 121   "Would a God who took": Ibid.

p. 123   "love loves unto purity": George MacDonald, "The Consuming Fire," in *Unspoken Sermons,* first series (Eureka, Calif.: Sunrise Book, 1988), p. 27.

p. 123   "He is always against sin": Ibid., p. 38, italics added.

p. 124   "Would a God who did not care": Packer, *Knowing God,* p. 143.

p. 125   "It is not a question": C. S. Lewis, *The Problem of Pain* (New York: Macmillan, 1962), p. 127.

p. 128   "The conditions of modern-day living": Richard Swenson, *Margin* (Colorado Springs: NavPress, 1992), p. 32.

Chapter 7: God Is Self-Sacrificing

p. 135   Athanasius, the bishop of Alexandria: Athanasius was present at the Council of Nicaea (A.D. 325), where the standard doctrine of the incarnation (Jesus was fully God and fully human) was defined. The later Nicene Creed is the orthodox (correct) understanding of the person of Jesus and the nature of the Trinity. During his lifetime Athanasius maintained that the doctrines established at Nicaea were correct, and firmly held his position against great opposition. He was exiled five times for his beliefs.

p. 135   I turned my questions . . . into a dialogue: The following dialogue is, of course, fictional. But the answers Athanasius gives are taken straight from the book *On the Incarnation.* In the interest of making it sound like an actual discussion, I have added some dialogue. But this was actually easy to do because Athanasius raises the questions I ask.

p. 141   "Why did the Father will [the crucifixion]?": Edward Yarnold, "The Theology of Christian Spirituality," in *The Study of Spirituality,* ed. Cheslyn Jones, Geoffrey Wainwright and Edward Yarnold (Oxford: Oxford University Press, 1986), p. 15.

p. 147   "The key, then, to loving God": Dallas Willard, *The Divine Conspiracy* (San Francisco: HarperSanFrancisco, 1998), p. 334.

Chapter 8: God Transforms

p. 152   "What could be more frustrating": David C. Needham, *Birthright* (Portland, Ore.: Multnomah Press, 1979), p. 69.

p. 153   "To be forgiven by God": L. Gregory Jones, *Embodying Forgiveness: A Theological Analysis* (Grand Rapids: Eerdmans, 1995), p. 159.

p. 156   This is why we struggle: *Regeneration* is a theological term used to describe the infusion of new life into the person who has been "born again."

p. 157   The word *flesh* (Greek *sarx*): I am intentionally using *sarx* instead of *flesh* because "flesh" is too closely associated with our physical bodies, which can lead to a too negative view of the body. I have also avoided using the NIV's "sinful nature" for *sarx,* because the idea of a "sinful nature" can lead people to assume that *sarx* is fundamental to our nature.

p. 157   The battle between *sarx* and spirit: Before coming to Christ we have no real conflict between *sarx* and Spirit—*sarx* is in complete control. But when we give ourselves to Christ and are indwelt by the Spirit the battle begins. Now our new identity is in conflict with the old identity. Even though we are new, the remains of our old identity are still very much with us.

p. 157   "Every babe in Christ is holy": John Wesley "On Sin in Believers," in *The Works of John Wesley* 3.4.3, 7, ed. Albert Outler, vol. 1 (Nashville: Abingdon, 1984).

p. 157   "For so long as we remain": John Calvin *Institutes of the Christian Religion* 4.15.11, ed. John T. McNeill (Philadelphia: Westminster Press, 1960).

p. 157   "inseparably linked to": Needham, *Birthright,* p. 79.

p. 158   "cuts off all watching": Wesley, *Works of John Wesley* 13.5.1.

p. 160   "'Christ in me' means": James S. Stewart, *A Man in Christ* (Vancouver: Regent College Publishing, 1935), p. 169.

p. 160   Country dogs and city dogs: I am indebted to Bob George and his ministry, People to People, for this illustration, which I heard at a Classic Christianity conference in 1993.

p. 161   "The spiritual life is not": Panayiotis Nellas, *Deification in Christ* (New York: St. Vladimir's Seminary Press, 1997), p. 136.

p. 163   "The question is not": Henri Nouwen, *In the Name of Jesus: Reflections on Christian Leadership* (New York: Crossroad, 2002), pp. 37-38.

p. 166   "When we go into solitude": Dallas Willard, foreword to *Invitation to Solitude and Silence,* by Ruth Haley Barton (Downers Grove, Ill.: InterVarsity Press, 2004), pp. 10-11.

p. 167   "We need to find God": This quote is taken from Jan Johnson's wonderful little Bible study *Solitude & Silence* (Downers Grove, Ill.: InterVarsity Press, 2003), p. 27.

pp. 168-69   Bible verses about identity in Christ: Many of these verses are excerpted from Neil Anderson's *Ministering the Steps to Freedom in Christ* (Ventura, Calif.: Gospel Light, 1998), p. 38. I have added a few.

Chapter 9: How to Make a Pickle

pp. 173-74   "We are a nation in love": Jeremy Rikfin, *Time Wars* (New York: Simon & Schuster, 1987), p. 71.

p. 174   "It is ironic that": Ibid., pp. 19-21.

p. 175   The clock was invented by monks: Sebastian De Grazia, *Of Time, Work and Leisure* (New York: Random House, 1994), p. 44.

p. 175   "Idleness is the enemy of the soul": *The Benedictine Handbook* (Norwich: Liturgical Press, 2003), p. 69.

p. 175   clock time began "gaining the upper hand": Carl Honoré, *In Praise of Slowness* (San Francisco: HarperSanFrancisco, 2004), p. 22.

p. 176   We "invented the machine": Ibid., p. 16.

p. 176   "In the past, man has been first": Nicholas Carr, "Is Google Making Us Stupid?" *The Atlantic,* July-August 2008, p. 62.

p. 176   "'Taylor's system' is still very much with us": Ibid.

p. 177   "tyranny of the urgent": See Charles E. Hummel, *Tyranny of the Urgent* (Downers Grove, Ill.: InterVarsity Press, 1994).

p. 178   In 1967, futurists told a Senate subcommittee: Richard A. Swenson, *Margin* (Colorado Springs: NavPress, 1992), p. 148.

p. 179   In a lifetime today's average person: Ibid., pp. 149-50.

p. 179   the average working parent: Honoré, *In Praise of Slowness*, p. 9.

p. 180   *One-Minute Bedtime Stories:* Ibid., p. 2.

p. 183   "Hurry," said Carl Jung: Quoted in Richard Foster's *Celebration of Discipline* (San Francisco: Harper & Row, 1978), p. 13.

p. 185   "In every waking hour": Robin R. Myers, *Morning Sun on a White Piano* (New York: Doubleday, 1998), p. 67.

p. 185   "Life is really nothing more": Richard Bailey and Joseph Carlson, *Slowing Down to the Speed of Life* (New York: HarperCollins, 1997) pp. 80-81, 164.

p. 186   "Spiritual renewal is": Taken from Miles J. Stanford, *Principles of Spiritual Growth* (Lincoln, Neb.: Back to the Bible Broadcast Publication, 1974), p. 13.

p. 186   "A student asked the President": Quoted in ibid., pp. 11-12.

p. 186   "The emerging picture": Malcolm Gladwell, *Outliers: The Story of Success* (New York: Little, Brown, 2008), p. 40.

p. 187   Mozart "developed late": Ibid., p. 41.

p. 189   "The deepest part of the soul": Robert Barron, *Heaven in Stone and Glass* (New York: Crossroad, 2000), p. 149.

p. 189   "Today the combat is not the same": Paul Evdokimov, *Ages of the Spiritual Life* (Crestwood, N.Y.: St. Vladimir's Seminary Press, 1998), p. 64, italics added.

p. 191   "It seems that most believers": Stanford, *Principles of Spiritual Growth,* p. 11.

acknowledgments

This book—and all of the books in The Apprentice Series—would not exist were it not for Dallas Willard, a living example of a true apprentice of Jesus, who has inspired me in countless ways. Dallas's outline of a "curriculum for Christlikeness" is the framework of these books. It is difficult to measure the impact of his life and writings on my soul.

And this book would not have been written were it not for Richard J. Foster, who has poured his life and wisdom into me for over twenty-five years. Everyone should have a teacher as brilliant and authentic as Richard—I am grateful. Thank you, Richard, for finding something in me worth believing in and taking a chance on.

The person that made the most sacrifice is my wonderful, beautiful, fun and very patient wife, Meghan Smith. She endured many months as a "writer's widow" and never complained. Thank you, Meghan, for knowing how important this series is to me by supporting and encouraging me every step of the way. And thanks for editing the material along the way. My whole life is better because of you. You still take my breath away.

My son and daughter, Jacob and Hope, also gave up a lot as I wrote.

Thank you for allowing me to tell your stories. Thanks too for being supportive throughout these years while I wrote, rewrote, edited and taught this material. I know that the time I spend with others is time taken from you. I will work to make it up to you!

I would also like to thank four former disciples and now colleagues for all of the encouragement and support they have given. The two "sons of thunder": Patrick Sehl, thank you for your relentless support and love for this material; and C. J. Fox, thanks for being an example of integrity and enthusiasm. The two "wise hobbits": Matt Johnson, thank you for your quiet confidence, dedication to the King and the kingdom, and scent of patchouli; and Jimmy Taylor, thanks for your creativity and depth, and sheer love of Jesus. These four young men are going to change the world.

I would like to thank three of my colleagues at Friends University who read the manuscript of The Apprentice Series, offered a lot of helpful suggestions and helped me avoid some errors—Dr. Chris Ketter for your theological insights, Dr. Stan Harstine for your biblical brilliance and Dr. Darcy Zabel for your literary skills.

I owe a great debt to Kathy Helmers, my agent and guide through the maze of publishing, for sharing my love for this series, shaping it into something good and then finding the right publishing partner. Kathy, you are the best at what you do, and I am fortunate to work with you.

I would also like to thank Jeff Crosby and Cindy Bunch of Inter-Varsity Press, who made it clear to me from the moment we met that you were quality people with incredible skills, a passion for publishing good books, and a clear vision for what this series is and can be. I am blessed to work with you both.

I would like to thank others who contributed in hidden ways.

Emil Johnson—for your careful reading of this book and endless encouragement.

Bob Casper—for your belief in me and these books, and for your brilliant mind.

Jeff Gannon—my pastor, friend and fellow worker in the kingdom.

Lyle SmithGraybeal—for never once having doubt about The Apprentice Series.

Vicki and Scott Price—for loving me and believing in this series.

Finally, thank you, thank you, thank you to those people who went through this "course" at Chapel Hill UMC, Wichita, Kansas, who studied and practiced the concepts in this series, and allowed me to learn from your experiences and insights. Your presence flows in the pages of the series. You worked hard on this material, and you deserve to be named: Betty Leader, Chris Faulk, Trevor Hinz, Stuart Mochrie, Doug Oliver, Ernie Reiger, Pete Orsi, Barb Orsi, Phil Ladwig, Richard Spillman, Arlo Casper, Marita Soucie, Tammy Langton, Craig Rhodes, Tracy Cassidy, Greg Fox, Michael Criss, Craig Warren, Ben Leader, Jane Albright, Chris McNeil, Joy McNeil, Paul Oldland, Denise Oldland, J. J. Miller, Charlotte Miller, Kelly Sooter, Steve Coen, David Nelson, Bob Casper, Nancy Wallace, Mary Warren, Shawn Chesser, Mary Uttig, Pam Tilson, Abe Rodriguez, Cassie Hill, Eric Johnson, Eva Johnson, Andrew Tash, C. J. Fox, Matt Johnson, Catherine Johnson, Bill Eichelberger, Laurie Rhodes, Sheree Gerig, Lu Ross, Bob Ross, Ashley Brockus, B. J. Brockus, Juliet Mochrie, Monica Coen, Jenny Bennett, Dan Bennett, Gary Shanks, Kylie Jennings, Arlene Amis, Kassie Taylor, Jason Searl, Carrie Mills, Preston Todd, Carlee Todd, Stacy Clark, Patrick Sehl, Janeen Sehl, Chuck Romig, Kim Romig, Scott Price, Vicki Price, Josh Luton, Carol Jones, Charlie Schwartz, Chrissy Searl, Christine Vogt, Holly Myers, Tony Myers, Jane Frye, Laurie Furse, Rick Furse, Lindsey Bricker, Pam Larsen, Suzanne Schwartz, Chris Randolph, Jill Casper, Mark Zonnefeld, Bob Epperson, Malaura Epperson, Charlie Tannehill, Cindy Tannehill, Dan Jehlik, Diana Storm, Jack Storm, Dick Heggestad, Cheryl Heggestad, Gay Hendrickson, Kim Packebush, Terri Guthrie, George Guthrie, Mike Todd, Terri Todd, Jennifer Hinz, Meghan Smith, Brooke Hill, Carol Fisher, Joan Tash, Brooke Krause, Dennis Phelps, Justin Lefto and Kara Lefto.

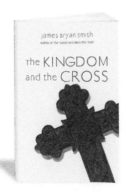

RENOVARÉ
www.renovare.org

Just over twenty years ago Richard J. Foster, my mentor and friend, said to me, "Jim, I'm starting a ministry. It is time for the walls to come down that separate denominations. The church needs to do better at its primary job—making disciples. And people need to learn how to practice the disciplines not just as individuals, but within groups. We need to help the modern church connect to the ancient church. I'd like you to help me design it and help lead it." I said yes. A month later we met for lunch and Richard told me he had come up with a name for this spiritual renewal ministry: Renovaré (ren-o-var-ay), a Latin word that means "to renew." I knew right away we were in trouble: no one could pronounce it, and no one knew what it meant. But it sounded really cool, because from the very start it was already doing what nobody else dared to.

What I like about Renovaré is that it comes alongside churches, resourcing them, without pretending to do their ultimate job: namely, making disciples of Jesus Christ. Many people forget that the followers of Christ were *disciples* because they practiced the *disciplines* of Christ; yet it was those practices of prayer, morality, sharing the gospel, service, Communion and spiritual gifts that made the disciples' lives so dynamic, and their spiritual lives so rich.

Renovaré is helping people and churches to rediscover these practices in order that we can be more like Jesus. I've worked with Renovaré for all these years (and partnered with them in the development of this book series) because they know that following Christ goes beyond denomination, even beyond the latest church program, and gives us tools to discover the with-God life in the very fabric of our everyday lives.

You may not immediately recognize it, but the book you have just read is very much a part of what Renovaré is all about—it has the same DNA as Renovaré, if you will. So I hope you don't stop here, because Renovaré—both as an organization and as a community of the most Christlike people I know—continues the conversation and the journey you have begun in this book. Come and walk with us.

God is stamping "aprentis" hearts with his kingdom purposes. He'll use *you* to change the world.

APRENTIS SERVES

Churches. Through a ministry of discipleship and formation, God can radically transform the way your church community lives and works and loves.

Like-minded leaders, organizations and thinkers. Collaborate with us to archive, engage and expand the field of Christian spiritual formation.

Students. Through an undergraduate degree track and second major in Christian spiritual formation, you can begin a serious life transformation through your college experience.

Begin an "apprentice" journey today.
For more information, contact the Aprentis Institute
at 316.295.5519 or email Aprentis@friends.edu.

Institute for Christian Spiritual Formation